# MASTERY TEACHING

MADELINE HUNTER

University of California, Los Angeles

TIP Publications
P. O. Box 514
El Segundo, CA 90245

## Other publications by the same author:

Motivation Theory for Teachers
Reinforcement Theory for Teachers
Retention Theory for Teachers
Teach More — Faster!
Teach for Transfer
Aide-ing in Education
Prescription for Improved Instruction
Improving Your Child's Behavior
Parent-Teacher Conferencing
Mastering Coaching and Supervision

Mastery Teaching
©Copyright 1982 by Madeline Hunter

Twenty-Seventh Printing, December, 1989
Twenty-Eighth Printing, August, 1990
Twenty-Ninth Printing, July, 1991
Thirtieth Printing, January 1992

ISBN 0-935567-09-7

Mastery Teaching Videotapes

A set of twenty, fifteen minute videotapes to accompany this book is available from Instructional Dynamics Inc., 845 Via de la Paz, Suite A177, Pacific Palisades, CA 90272.

To Margaret Devers,
the superb administrative assistant
who supported and assisted me for
twenty years as I grew in knowledge
about teaching and learning,
this book is gratefully and fondly
dedicated.

# TABLE OF CONTENTS

# PREFACE

This book and its accompanying series of *Mastery Teaching Videotapes* were developed to increase the teaching effectiveness of those who work with teen-agers and young adults. Of course, as students mature we expect them to assume increasing responsibility for their own learning. As teachers "mature," it is equally their responsibility to increase those professional skills which research has demonstrated will accelerate the learning of all students. This book and set of videotapes present some teaching techniques that are applicable to all disciplines, all learners, all methodologies, and all teaching styles and personalities.

Appreciation is expressed to Dr. Andrea Rich and Dr. Vera Martinez of the UCLA Office of Instructional Development for their financial and administrative support, to Bill Wolf, Hamid Natily and Peter Prager of the Instructional Media Center for their technical and artistic expertise, and to Margaret Devers and Lillian Ostroff whose secretarial assistance made manuscripts and videoscripts become realities.

The ultimate reality of this venture will be your accelerating teaching effectiveness with resultant increases in successful and satisfying learning accomplishment by your students.

# INTRODUCTION

In this book and the accompanying set of *Mastery Teaching Videotapes*, you will find described many teaching techniques you are already using. We learned these techniques from watching effective teachers teach. We have labeled these techniques and explained the psychological theory behind why they work. As a result, from now on ycu will know what you are doing when you teach, why you are doing what you do, and do that consciously and deliberately to increase your students' learning. In no way have we included all the techniques which make teachers more effective. However, as you read and view, you will find that you may add some new techniques to your repertoire of effective teaching skills.

The book and tapes of *Mastery Teaching* were designed to be used for either group discussion or individual study to increase teaching effectiveness. A study guide or meeting plan precedes each chapter. Because both viewing and reading are included, you must be the decision maker as to whether the suggested plan is appropriate for you or whether an activity of your own design might better serve your purpose. The chapters in the book and the tapes have been organized in a logical sequence. No one chapter or tape, however, is dependent on your having read or viewed another; so you may decide to "mix and match." As long as you have a reason for doing what you're doing, feel free to innovate, but remember that innovation is not good in and of itself without a reason for change.

If you are using this material with a group, usually it is facilitating to determine a group leader (appointed, elected or volunteer). That person should have the opportunity to read the chapter and view the videotape before the discussion so (s)he can recognize and highlight facilitating contributions from group members and be ready with some examples to "prime the pump" should the participants have difficulty in generating them. It also helps to have someone with advance knowledge available so any misunderstandings or confusion can be cleared.

If, as a result of your interaction with the ideas and techniques that are presented, you find your teaching is not only more effective but also is more satisfying to you and your students, this book and videotapes will have served their purpose.

*Madeline Hunter*

# I  DECISIONS IN TEACHING

Guide for Group Discussion or Individual Study

**Objectives:**           *Participants will:*
a. List three categories of decisions in teaching.
b. State generalizations which should be considered in making decisions in each category.
c. Identify their own decisions in each category for a subsequent class.

**Anticipatory Set:**     "If you had to group all the teaching decisions you make in just three categories, what would those categories be?"

**Input & Modeling:**     Read the chapter and/or view the videotape, "Decisions in Teaching."

**Checking Understanding & Guided Practice:**     Identify the category of each of the following decisions as:
I.   Content,
II.  Behavior of the learner, or
III  Behavior of the teacher.

Write the number by each statement so it can be compared with the answers. (When finished, someone might call out the number of the question and the group compare answers by holding up one, two or three fingers.)

*The teacher is deciding whether:*
A. The content should be Chaucer or Shakespeare.
B. To stand by a student to increase that student's concern or move to the other side of the room to lower concern.
C. To tell students they need not worry if at first things are not clear because everyone has trouble initially.
D. To have students write a paper or take a test to demonstrate their understanding.
E. To have students validate their comprehension by making a diorama or a time line.

F. To start with the ideas of Socrates or those of Plato.
G. To have students read the chapter or view a film.
H. To teach photosynthesis or respiration.
I. To praise a student for what he has accomplished or chide him for what he has not.
J. To teach by using examples in the book or to create original examples.
K. To have students learn from discussing or from experimenting.
L. To indicate the number correct on a student's paper or the number incorrect.
M. To teach the critical attributes of assumptions and conclusions.

### Answers

A-I    Content
B-III   Behavior of the teacher
C-III   Behavior of the teacher
D-II    Behavior of the learner (output)
E-II    Behavior of the learner (output)
F-I     Content
G-II    Behavior of the learner (input)
H-I    Content
I-III    Behavior of the teacher
J-III    Behavior of the teacher
K-II    Behavior of the learner (input)
L-III   Behavior of the teacher
M-I    Content

Identify the decisions you are making for your next class session as:

I. Content,
II. Behavior of the learner, or
III. Behavior of the teacher.

If you are working in a group, check your decisions with another group member. If you are working by yourself, jot them down so you can inspect them after your class session to see if your predictions materialized.

**Independent Practice:** Apply this information as you plan for subsequent classes.

# DECISIONS IN TEACHING

Educators have finally arrived at the point that professionals in medicine achieved when the latter discovered that germs and not evil spirits were causing much of the problem. We now know many cause-effect relationships in teaching and learning. As a result, we can use those causal relationships to promote student learning in the same way the doctor uses his medical knowledge to promote health. In both education and medicine we are learning more each day even though there still remains much we don't know.

Whenever humans are involved, we are dealing with probability, not certainty. When the doctor prescribes, it is to increase the probability of the patient's recovery, not to guarantee it. In the same way, if teaching decisions and actions are based on the principles presented in this book and in the *Mastery Teaching* series of videotapes, the probability of students' learning will be increased, but it will not be guaranteed.

There is no question but that genetic endowment and past experience influence students' learning, but your own teaching decisions also have a powerful impact. Consequently, teaching is now defined as a *constant stream of professional decisions made before, during and after interaction with the student: decisions which, when implemented, increase the probability of learning*. Students learn more when they are taught effectively than they can learn on their own. *Even champions have coaches.*

For the last two decades, educators at the University of California, Los Angeles, have been studying teaching decisions and their implementation: the essence of the process of teaching. They found that regardless of who or what is being taught, all teaching decisions fall into three categories: (1) what content to teach next, (2) what the student will do to learn and to demonstrate learning has occurred, and (3) what the teacher will do to facilitate the acquisition of that learning. When those professional decisions are made on the basis of sound psychological theory and *if* those decisions also reflect the teacher's sensitivity to the student and to the situation, *learning will be increased.* Should errors be made in any of those three decisions, student learning can be impeded. Consequently, it is important for teachers to identify consciously and deliberately the decisions needing to be made in each category and base their decisions on research-validated knowledge. Equally important is teachers' ability to "read" signals from students and to assess the learning situation so necessary adjustments will be made.

3

## I The Content Decision

The first professional decision to be made is the answer to the question, "What will be taught?" You may be thinking that decision has already been made. You're to teach English I, History of the United States, French II, or Computer Science. Those subjects merely label the content area in which you, the teacher, need to make the critical decision about the particular part of that content you will teach *today*. To increase the probability of students' learning, that decision must reflect your knowledge of what that particular group of students already knows and what is next to be learned. The psychological generalization which guides your content decision is that basic concepts, simple generalizations and processes must be acquired before more complex learnings are achieved. Advanced processes and understandings are built on a pyramid of simpler ones.

  complex understandings and processes

simpler generalizations and skills

simple concepts and behaviors

Therefore, to make the decision about the content you are going to teach successfully tomorrow, you need to determine which prior learnings are prerequisite to more complex ones and make sure those essential learnings have been *acquired* by your students (not "have been presented to") before advanced material is introduced.

Once the decision has been made about the "what" of teaching, the content decision, teacher and student effort should be directed to the acquisition of that new level of learning, not be dissipated on nonessential or tangential matters. It is tempting to spend class time on vivid or interesting "bird walks" that may distract attention from, rather than enhance understanding of, more important issues. A typical example is, "By the way, that reminds me of something that happened _____."
If "what happened" will help students understand what is being presented, by all means use the example. If "what happened" is tangential or only loosely related, don't waste time by introducing it. If you have loads of extra time or comedy relief needs to be introduced to brighten up the lesson, a "bird walk" might be forgivable, but most of us find that time and energy are in too short supply to be expended on loosely associated material or random exchange between students and teachers. This does not mean you ignore students' nonrelevant

comments. It is a sign of skill in teaching to dignify a student's extraneous contribution without letting it dilute the lesson. "That's an interesting point that will come a little later," usually will handle a tangential contribution.

Then by all means *do* come to it later, either with that student after class or with the group at a time when it is relevant. "You remember Harry cited an example of _____."

Lest you think disciplining yourself in terms of your content decision imposes rigidity on your teaching, it doesn't. It adds the professional rigor that leads to successful learning. Remember, *you're the decision maker;* and if, during class, a *better* idea emerges, by all means pursue it.

You may wish to delegate the content decision to your students and let them decide when they have achieved sufficient mastery to move on. However, as their teacher, you can't delegate your responsibility for the results of that decision and for its potential to increase or interfere with the probability of their learning.

## II The Decision Regarding Learning Behavior of the Student

While the first decision of teaching is based on content, the *what* of teaching, the second decision is directed to the *student behavior* that makes learning possible, the student's *how* of learning. There are two aspects of a student's learning behavior. One aspect is focused on the input modalities the student will use to acquire knowledge or skill. Will (s)he read, discuss, listen, observe, and/or do? *There is no one best way to learn,* and use of a combination of these input behaviors usually is more effective then relying on only one.

Another aspect of the teacher's decision about learning behavior is focused on students' output which validates acquisition of the knowledge or skill. That output must be *perceivable* so you know (not hope) that students have achieved and are ready to move on to the next learning or whether you must reteach or extend practice of the current learning. Also, that student output behavior must *validate* that learning has been accomplished. Output can't be such that students can bluff, guess, or be lucky in their demonstration of accomplishment. As with the content decision, the input and output student behavior decision also can be delegated to students but *not* your responsibility for the results of their decision.

Your *instructional objective* specifies the first two teaching decisions of 1) content and 2) behavior of the learner and brings both of them to the level of conscious, professional decision making rather than leaving them as vague intentions or wishful thinking.

To make those two decisions more identifiable, in the examples below, the specific content is capitalized, and the validating student behavior is written in italics. All instructional objectives begin with, "The Learner will (T.L.w.)—."

T.L.w. *state* the SIX CATEGORIES OF PLANTS and *describe* the CHARACTERISTICS OF EACH.

T.L.w. *write* his/her INTERPRETATION OF ARNOLD'S POEM.

T.L.w. *respond in German* to the QUESTIONS ON PAGE 37.

T.L.w. *diagram* the ASSERTIONS AND CONCLUSION.

T.L.w. *discuss* the CHANGES WHICH RESULTED FROM THE TREATY.

T.L.w. *solve* the QUADRATIC EQUATIONS ON PAGE 97.

Having an articulated instructional objective, rather than intuitive or subliminal intent, accomplishes two things. First, it helps you focus your teaching on the learning behavior which you will use to validate whether students have achieved the intended learning. Second, it encourages you to identify the prerequisite learnings which must be taught (and learned!) in order for students to achieve the intended results.

### III  The Decision Regarding Teacher Behavior

The third decision in teaching (note that this is the *third* decision, not the first) is directed to your own teaching behavior: what *you* will do to increase learning. If you deliberately use principles of learning which research indicates are accelerants to student achievement, you will have power to increase your students' motivation to learn, the speed and the amount (rate and degree) of their learning, and their retention and appropriate transfer of that learning to new situations requiring creativity, problem solving, and decision making. Principles of learning constitute a powerful pharmacy of alternatives from which you can create an effective learning prescription. Knowing principles of learning and deliberately and artistically using them are the hallmarks of the master teacher. This book and the accompanying series of *Mastery Teaching Videotapes* were developed to present some of these principles to you and thereby to help you consciously achieve master teaching.

The responsibility for making these three decisions of, (1) content (what to teach today and tomorrow), (2) behavior of the learners (which input modalities students are going to utilize and the student output that will validate successful accomplishment), and (3) your teaching behavior (utilization of principles of learning to accelerate achievement) sounds like a lot of professional decision making. It is! These decisions, however, are already being made by you either purposefully, intuitively, or by default every day you teach. As you read, you will find that you already are using much of what is described in this book or shown in the *Mastery Teaching Videotapes;* but now you will have categories; and labels for the decisions you are making, and you will know the research that supports them. You may also learn some new techniques which will make your teaching not only easier but more predictably successful.

Each chapter in this book and each module in the videotape series will focus on some aspect of professional decision making to help you become more conscious of why you do what you are doing. As a result, you will become increasingly effective as a teacher.

After you study this book and view the videotapes, you should have deliberately constructed a professional launching pad from which your own particular style and artistry in teaching can soar.

Bon voyage!

## II   INCREASING THEIR MOTIVATION
### PART I

Guide for Group Discussion or Individual Study

**Objectives:**

*Participants will:*
a. List techniques they use to increase motivation.
b. Label items on the list according to categories.
c. Generate examples in any neglected category.
d. Try motivational techniques in subsequent classes.

**Anticipatory Set:**

List 5-10 things you might do in your classroom to increase students' motivation or intent to learn.

**Input & Modeling:**

Read the chapter and/or view the videotape, "Motivation Part I."

**Checking Understanding & Guided Practice:**

List three factors that affect motivation and give classroom examples of the use of each. Examine your original list and mark with a C those items which would raise or lower students' level of concern. Mark a P, N, or U by those items which involve pleasant, unpleasant, or neutral feeling tones and mark with an S those items which will increase a student's successful accomplishment. There will be some items which are not discrete but will fall into several categories. There may be other items which don't seem to fit the categories you have learned about. Don't worry about those (we're introducing neutral feeling tones); you'll learn the labels of additional motivational factors in the next chapter. If you have no items in any one of the three categories (Concern, Feeling Tone, or Success), this may alert you to the fact that you could be neglecting an important motivational propellant in your classroom. Try to generate some items in that category that you predict might be successful with your students. Compare your items with those of other group members. While each of you has a different teaching style and personality, it is amazing how your repertoire of motivational behaviors can increase as you deliberately incorporate new ideas into your teaching plans.

**Independent Practice:** Try some new ideas in your class. Some will fit your style and/or students better than others. Make sure, however, that you don't narrow your repertoire. Keep adding to it.

Keep your original list because in the next chapter you'll learn to label additional, research-based ways in which you can affect students' motivation to learn.

# INCREASING THEIR MOTIVATION
## PART I

Motivation, a student's *intent* to learn, is one of the most important factors in successful accomplishment. All teachers suffer frustration when a student is not putting forth effort to learn. Students may even face us with a stance of "Go ahead and teach; you don't bother me none," a statement made to the writer by an "unmotivated" student.

It is important we realize, 1) that motivation is not generic; it is learned, 2) that what is learned can be taught, and 3) that teaching is our business. Therefore, we need to become knowledgeable about, and skilled in the use of, professional techniques which have high potential for increasing a student's motivation or intent to learn.

Many factors affecting motivation are beyond our control. Students' families, neighborhoods, former teachers, or previous experiences in the same content have all had an effect on the motivation of students in our classes. Those factors are beyond our control. They have already occurred and are part of students' past. It's only in the *present* that we can make changes; thus, we need to become skilled in the use of six factors which we can modify daily in our classrooms: factors which have the power to increase students' effort and intent to learn.

No one of these six factors is most powerful, nor are they completely discrete. They are like the digestive, circulatory and endocrine systems of the body. There is constant interaction. By adjusting one factor, however, you may restore balance to the entire system.

## I Level of Concern

One factor you can affect in the classroom is the student's *level of concern* about achieving the learning. How much does the student care about whether he or she learns?

In the past, we believed that stress or concern was undesirable. Now we know that a moderate level of concern is essential to an individual's putting forth effort. If you are satisfied with your appearance, job, or where you live, you will not put forth effort to change it. It is only when you become concerned that you will "do something."

For example, when things seem to be going well in your class, what are you motivated to change? Nothing! It is only when you become concerned about new techniques you feel you should learn, or you wish something different to result from your teaching, or another teacher is producing better results, or you are being considered for tenure, or your superior indicates all is not well, that you begin to look for ways to increase your instructional effectiveness. Should your concern become too high, however, your energy may be diverted from instructional growth to dealing with your concern for self-maintenance or even, at times, survival..

The psychological generalization which guides our teaching decisions is: *A moderate level of concern stimulates effort to learn.* When there is no concern, there is little or no learning. When there is too much concern, there may be no energy available for learning.

You are already utilizing this principle of learning (possibly intuitively) and raising or lowering students' concern when you:

a. Stand next to a student who is not participating to raise concern, or move away from an anxious student to lower concern.

b. Announce that, "This will probably be on the test," or reassure your class that, "Everyone has trouble with this at first, but, as we work, it will become increasingly clear."

c. Give a test that you grade, or give a test followed by the answers so students can check their own learning.

d. Announce that, "This part is difficult and a high level of concentration and effort is required," or that, "This is difficult, but we will work on it for several days before you are expected to know it."

e. Give a "whooping" final exam which counts for most of the grade or give many mini exams where one low grade will not be so significant.

One difference between the predictably effective teacher and the intuitive teacher is that the former consciously and deliberately raises or lowers the concern of the group or of individual students when a change in level of concern is needed to increase learning effort.

## II Feeling Tone

The way a student feels in a particular situation affects the amount of effort (s)he is willing to put forth to achieve learning. Feeling tones exist on a continuum which extends from pleasant through neutral to unpleasant. Obviously, students are most inclined to put forth effort to learn if they find the learning situation pleasant and if they anticipate they will be successful (a pleasant feeling). Common sense as well as research would tell us to make our classroom environment a pleasant one where students have high probability of achieving success. This book and the *Mastery Teaching Videotapes* were designed to assist you to accomplish this objective.

Unpleasant feeling tones also activate a learner to put forth effort. ("If that isn't finished, there will be undesirable consequences.") Most of us are reluctant to use unpleasant feeling tones in our classrooms. The reason is that, although unpleasant feeling tones are effective in stimulating effort, they can have undesirable side effects. The student may learn, but also may avoid that content or teacher in the future. Each of us has had the experience of learning something with unpleasant feelings (stoves burn, Latin conjugations, English grammar, statistics). We got through the ordeal, and we may still remember what we learned, but we have avoided that situation or content ever since.

While we need to be aware of and occasionally utilize the power of unpleasant feeling tones (when pleasant ones aren't working), we should strive to eliminate the possible aftereffect of student avoidance by returning to pleasant feeling tones as soon as students put forth effort to learn.

Examples:

"I've really put a lot of pressure on you, and you've responded magnificently."

"In spite of your struggle with these concepts, you've emerged with a clear understanding of them."

"I know you were angry about the demands being made, but you should be proud of the improvement in your performance."

"Many of you have felt discouraged and wanted to give up, but your perseverance has paid off."

Neutral feeling tones (neither pleasant nor unpleasant) are void of motivational propulsion. Neutral feelings are useful, however, to terminate an unproductive or unpleasant situation so that, later, we can return to the task with pleasant feelings.

Examples:

"Everyone is tired and confused; so let's forget it today and work on it at another time when we're fresh."

"Don't worry if you missed several; it won't count on your grade, and you now know what you need to study."

"This is our first attempt; so don't be concerned if you don't understand. We'll need to do several before it will be clear to you."

Your professional task is to determine whether it would be more productive, in terms of students' intent to put forth learning effort, for them to experience pleasant, unpleasant, or neutral feeling tones. No one feeling is always the most productive. An awareness of the three feeling tones and facility in creating each of them, when needed, are the hallmarks of a teacher who is proactive on students' motivation rather than merely being reactive to their lack of it.

### III Success

A third factor which increases students' motivation is the feeling of success. In order to feel successful, one must expend effort and have a certain degree of uncertainty about the outcome. We do not feel successful when we put forth little effort for accomplishment. If we turn the knob and the door opens, we feel no elation. We predicted that would happen. If the door is jammed and, by exerting skill and effort, we manage to open it, we feel successful.

It is the same with learning. If the task is easy and requires little effort, we feel little success and are not motivated to continue. If, with effort and with no guarantee we can accomplish the learning, we achieve it, we feel successful and usually are motivated to try to do more.

You may wonder how you can affect students' successful achievement. Isn't that a result of students' ability and effort? In part, yes. But student success is also responsive to two other factors which you control. The first is the level of difficulty of the learning task, something you can adjust because you set the task. The second factor is your teaching skill which will make students' learning more probable. This book and series of videotapes should increase your skill in deliberate use of elements that make you an increasingly effective teacher.

You might think of successful achievement as clearing an "intellectual" high jump bar. A high jump can be made easier or more difficult as the bar is lowered or raised. For the Olympic champion, it should be set just above the level where success is reasonably predictable. Clearing the bar it is not certain; it will require effort. The champion will be challenged to try, and he will feel successful as he clears it. If the bar is set too low, even if the champion jumps (which he probably won't bother to do), there will be no feeling of success because there was certainty that it would be cleared. Champions don't continue to jump a bar "that anyone could get over."

On the other hand, short-legged, stubby Kenny won't even make an attempt if the bar is set high. He's sure he can't clear it so he's "unmotivated" to try. If the bar is lowered to the point where he thinks he has a reasonable chance of clearing it, he may be motivated to attempt it. As he experiences success, the bar can be raised, and he'll continue his effort.

The more success students have experienced in the past, the more optimistic they are about future performance. Even if there is a greater risk of failure, successful students will try. On the other hand, the more they have failed in the past, the less willing students are to expose themselves to risk because their prediction is that they won't make it.

Therefore, to protect themselves, they won't try. They are "unmotivated."

Consequently, we need to lower that "academic bar" for less able students. *This does not mean we "let them get by with less"* but that we build in the support and assistance needed so they can clear that educational bar and try for the next higher one. As an example, so all students experience success, we can direct our easier first questions to the less able students. We direct difficult questions to more able students, and then we may ask our less able students, who now have heard the answers, to restate those answers in different words, a demanding but less risky task. (And a task that will give them the repetition necessary for future success.)

Teachers of teenagers and young adults are learning to raise and lower the "academic bar" by working with smaller groups within the class while the rest of the class is working independently (something that is common in elementary schools where students have much less ability to work independently). Working with groups within a class enables the teacher to give additional help and to raise and lower the academic challenge to meet differing student needs, thereby using the factor of successful accomplishment to increase students' motivation to learn.

Again, let us remind you that no one factor, *concern, feeling tone, or success* is most important. They interact, and we use them in concert. If there is some risk but not too much, the student experiences mild concern. When that student is successful, pleasant feeling tones result.

As you consciously use a stimulating level of concern (enough to get students to put forth effort but not so much that it diverts energy), as you deliberately create pleasant feeling tones (if they do not work, you may need to use slightly unpleasant ones and, after the student is energized, return to pleasant), and as your teaching makes success as a result of effort not only possible but probable, you will exert a major influence on your students' motivation to learn.

In the next chapter, you will learn additional factors that you can adjust within your classroom to affect students' motivation to learn.
to learn.

# III INCREASING THEIR MOTIVATION
## PART II

Guide for Group Discussion or Individual Study

**Objectives:**

*Participants will:*

a. State three additional elements they can change in their classrooms to increase students' motivation to learn and generate examples of each.

b. Experiment in subsequent teaching with all six possibilities for increasing students' motivation to learn and then select for future use those which appear to be most effective.

**Anticipatory Set:**

Recall from the last chapter three ways to increase students' motivation or intent to learn. Look at your original list of things you might do in your class and locate the items you couldn't label.

**Input & Modeling:**

Read the chapter and/or view the videotape, "Motivation Part II."

**Checking Understanding & Guided Practice:**

List the three additional elements (Interest, Knowledge of Results, Extrinsic-Intrinsic Motivation) and generate examples of each which could be effective with your students. Examine your next teaching objective and generate techniques in each of the six categories of motivation that you might use in your next class session. You probably won't use all of them, but this activity will give you the opportunity of selecting from a repertoire of alternatives those you predict will be most effective. This type of decision making is the essence of the process of teaching.

**Independent Practice:** In your next class try the techniques you selected. The reactions of the students will help you further refine your effectiveness in influencing students' efforts to learn. All of us tend to get in a rut and repeat what has worked for us in the past; so occasionally go back and reread the two chapters on motivation and/or review the videotapes so you are taking advantage of the full repertoire of motivational possibilities rather than majoring in only a few.

# INCREASING THEIR MOTIVATION
## PART II

In the last chapter, you learned about three factors which a teacher can do something about and which affect students' motivation: 1) level of concern, 2) feeling tone, and 3) success. This chapter will identify three additional factors. Remember that no one factor is most important and often they work in concert. By changing only one or two factors, however, we can make a tremendous difference in students' intent to learn.

### IV Interest

The fourth factor which has been demonstrated to affect a student's intention to learn is *interest* in the learning task. Interest is not inborn but is acquired. Interest can be promoted by the teacher in two ways. The first is by utilizing students' interest in themselves. Relating material to be learned to the student's life, use of the student's name, use of examples that refer to students or experiences in the class, and positive statements about students' performance or their learning ability are only a few possibilities which a creative teacher can use to make material more interesting.

    Examples:

        "Suppose John, here, were presenting an argument for electing his friend and Charles wished to challenge his position..."

        "If we were to increase the percentage of A's in this class by..."

        "Mary, here, has the pigmentation most commonly associated with Nordic races while Sue's is more typical of the Latinos."

        "Let's each make a chart of the ear lobes of our next generation if we were to marry a person with _____."

A second way we can make material more interesting is by accentuating the novel or vivid: that which is different or unexpected. We can achieve novelty in our classrooms by such simple devices as a change in our voice or our position in the room, from lecturing to questioning, from teacher decisions to student decisions, from written to oral reports, and/or from texts to films. Anything different from what is usually experienced can elicit an "alerting reflex" in the student's brain and greater attention results. Nothing continues to remain "different," however; habituation results, and the student may no longer be attracted to the "new thing." Consequently, we must take advantage of the alerting reflex to TEACH so the material begins to have value on its own merit, not because it's novel. Just a little novelty usually will do the trick of eliciting attention. Too much vividness or flamboyance can actually distract from the learning.

Another way we can make learning vivid is by stressing the novel aspect or the differentness of the material itself.

Examples:

"The property that makes a fungus different from every other plant is that, like a human, it can't manufacture its own food but must get it from some other source."

"Let's look at these assertions: 1) Students who don't study always get better grades, 2) The more boring the book, the easier it is to remember."

"The results of this experiment will really surprise you."

A combination of novelty and relating the learning to the student will capture students' interest and therefore increase their motivation to learn.

Examples:

"When you order your favorite McDonald's milkshake, it won't melt even if you heat it in the oven. That's the result of an emulsifier made from the algae we're studying."

"Suppose you believed in reincarnation. In your next life what would you need to accomplish that you didn't accomplish satisfactorily in this life?"

"You are going to make up your own test. Ask three questions that you believe would really check a person's understanding of the chapter and then answer them. Your grade will reflect the quality of your questions as well as the answers."

"Discuss three important skills you need to develop to make you more effective."

Almost everything we teach can be related to something in the student's own life, thereby making that content more interesting. Even if there is no novelty in the content itself, the *way* we present it, *what* the students do with it and *how* they let us know they have learned it, can be different from mundane expectations in classrooms which hold little novelty—only more of the same.

A caution needs to be sounded so we don't make things so novel or vivid that students focus only on the novelty and not on the content. Students (and sometimes we) can get so intrigued by the novelty, we forget that the reason it was introduced was to increase students' motivation to learn that which was not novel. The writer watched one teacher demonstrating part-whole relationships with a luscious cake.

Students' minds were so engaged with the final disposition of the cake (wishfully, in their stomachs) that they missed the fractional understandings of the lesson.

An effective guideline is: *Use novelty and vividness to attract students' attention to learning, not to distract from the learning.*

### V Knowledge of Results

A fifth and very powerful element we can change in our classrooms is the amount, specificity, and immediacy of the feedback students receive about their performance: *their knowledge of results.*

Just doing something again, without knowing how well we did it, is not very satisfying or stimulating. As a result, we are not motivated to continue or improve our performance. When we find out what we are doing well, what needs to be improved, and most importantly, *what to do to improve it* and then feel that there is reasonable probability *that we can improve it,* we are motivated to try to accomplish that improvement.

Grades usually are neither immediate nor specific enough to give adequate knowledge of results. An "A" or "B" simply informs the student, "Don't worry; you're doing O.K." The student, however, does not know what part was O.K. or whether one part was superb and other parts need to be improved. Motivation, the intent to put forth effort, will increase if the student has *specific* knowledge of results. "Your ideas are excellent. Now you need to give examples of how they would look if implemented," encourages the student to carry his/her inspiration into application. "You seem to know the content, but you need to organize it into sequential relationships. For example, you might, _____," stimulates the student to organize and categorize. "Your use of examples is superb; now you need to draw generalizations from them," encourages the student to move from specifics to conclusions. Each of these comments has infinitely more motivational potential than an "A" or a "B" grade.

It takes more time to put comments on a student's paper than it does to write that terminal grade. Therefore, we suggest, to save your time and energy and to increase your own motivation to use knowledge of results in your classes, that you use class participation with immediate feedback plus frequent, *brief* tests and papers for students' responses (see the chapter on "Checking Students' Understanding"). A one page (or less) paper not only requires students to tighten their thinking (they can't "run off at the pen"), but it enables you to go quickly over a set of class papers and return them with immediate and specific knowledge of results that can motivate students to improve their thinking as well as the product of that thinking.

Your students also can receive knowledge of results as you beam a question to the whole class, give them several answers from which they choose (a verbal multiple choice situation), and then give them the correct answer with *the reason it is correct*. This teaching technique gives knowledge of results with no public humiliation for those who were incorrect and gives a feeling of success plus pleasant feeling tones to those who responded correctly.

## VI Intrinsic-Extrinsic Motivation

No doubt, as you read about these five motivational factors which every teacher can change in the classroom (level of concern, feeling tones, success, interest, and knowledge of results) you are wondering what happened to *intrinsic* motivation: the student's supplying his/her own propulsion to learn. Needless to say, if students are intrinsically motivated and show up in our class pleading, "Teach me. I'm ready!" we can forget everything in this chapter. Unfortunately, that usually is not the case.

Intrinsic and extrinsic motivation exist as opposite ends of a continuum which represents the relationship of the learning to the goal achieved. Completely intrinsic motivation exists when satisfaction from the activity is the student's primary goal. The student does something in order to enjoy the activity of "doing it." When a student is learning in order to achieve some result from having accomplished that learning (an "A," getting the course over with, meeting a requirement, becoming knowledgeable in that content), (s)he is operating from more extrinsic motivation. *Intrinsic* motivation is not necessarily saintly, nor is *extrinsic* motivation sinful. Both are effective. The difference is that with intrinsic motivation you are doing something because you wish to do it. Satisfaction comes from engaging in the learning process. The more you learn, the more satisfaction you receive, and the more you want to learn. Consequently, intrinsic motivation is self-perpetuating. Hobbies and games (when winning is not the objective) are typical examples of intrinsic motivation where the process rather than the product is the primary goal.

When you are exerting effort because of extrinsic motivation, once the goal is achieved (you passed the course, you finished the paper, you took the test) you no longer have the goal as an extrinsic motivator so effort ceases. *Unless*, while you were putting forth effort, you were, 1) somewhat concerned about the outcome; yet you experienced 2) the pleasant feeling tone of being 3) successful, and you found the material 4) interesting, novel, and related to your own life. Then, if a teacher gave you 5) immediate and specific knowledge of results about what you had accomplished and helped you to continue to improve your performance, there is high probability that you enjoyed the whole process and your motivation moved from being completely extrinsic toward the intrinsic end of the continuum. You're motivated to "do it some more" because you enjoyed it.

Many of us are concerned because our students are extrinsically motivated. It is important to remember that a great deal of what each of us does every day is also extrinsically motivated. We get up, go to work, hand in reports, grade papers, take inservice classes and read books such as this one, not because we find intrinsic pleasure in each of these activities, but because they will enable us to achieve the goal of being an increasingly competent professional. If we find that the pursuit of teaching excellence becomes an exciting and rewarding pastime, we'll become more intrinsically motivated to reread this book, review the *Mastery Teaching Videotapes* and seek other sources continually to increase our instructional effectiveness.

One result of efforts to learn about motivation will be increased awareness of factors that increase students' motivation so we'll change from intuitive or random use to deliberate inclusion of six motivational factors in teaching: to move students from completely extrinsic motivation (they have to learn it) to more intrinsic motivation (they enjoy learning it). The increased learning dividends to students will guarantee escalating intrinsic motivation for our own professional growth.

# IV   GETTING STUDENTS SET TO LEARN

Guide for Group Discussion or Individual Study

**Objectives:**
*Participants will:*
a. State three ways to use prime time in their classes.
b. Generate activities that are productive in terms of student learning, which can be used during "class keeping" chores.
c. Generate activities that will develop productive anticipatory sets for subsequent class periods.

**Anticipatory Set:**
Respond to these questions:
1. How important to students' learning are the first few minutes of class? Why do you think so?
2. As a result of your belief, what advice would you give to teachers regarding those first few minutes?

**Input & Modeling:**
Read the chapter and/or view the videotape, "Getting Students Set to Learn."

**Checking for Understanding & Guided Practice:**
Review the two questions in terms of validating or modifying some of your first answers.

Generate a list of activities you could use in your class while handling administrative or housekeeping matters. (Notice that each study guide in this series begins with an anticipatory set and you are given the objectives of each chapter.)

Identify the objective for your next class. Generate some anticipatory sets that might be used to (a) focus students on the learning, (b) give them some practice that would help them accomplish it, and (c) give you some diagnostic information about their entry knowledge.

Determine how you will let students know the objective of your next class and why it is important for them to achieve.

**Independent Practice:**

Try your ideas in class. Remember, even if these techniques are not new to you, consciously thinking about them may be. As a result, you may not be as fluent or comfortable using them initially as you will when these teaching techniques become automatic.

# GETTING STUDENTS SET TO LEARN

First impressions are important, and the beginning of your class is no exception. You have experienced how important first impressions of people or places can be. Research in learning validates that effect. Information introduced at the beginning of any sequence is more easily learned and better remembered than equally difficult material encountered later in that same sequence. This generalization is true, all other factors being equal, regardless of whether the sequence is a list of words, a group of concepts or generalizations, the pages of a chapter, the class period, or a week or a month of instruction. Obviously, when certain material is more vivid, more meaningful or more interesting, it will be more easily learned and remembered regardless of its position in a sequence.

We need to take advantage of the learning propulsion inherent in the beginning of our class and not waste that beginning "prime time" on "soap opera activity." Prime time can be wasted while we wait for the stragglers to arrive, while we take roll, collect or pass out papers, correct homework which isn't essential to today's lesson, make announcements that aren't that important or don't have to be made in prime time, or while we engage in other "administrivia." Such activities often are better placed later in the period when they won't "burn up" that powerful beginning time. If something other than today's content must be taken care of at the beginning of class, it can be combined with important learning activities by using the following techniques:

## Review

1. Direct a review question to the entire class. Take part of the roll or pass out some papers while all students are thinking about the answer, and then call on a student whom you anticipate will give the correct answer. Then ask another question and use students' thinking time to continue your "housekeeping" or "class keeping" chores. By using beginning time in this way, each student has the opportunity (and the obligation) of formulating an answer in his/her own mind and then checking what is heard against what was thought. Correction of unvoiced misunderstandings or erroneous answers can be accomplished without visibility or embarrassment.

2. Ask students to write something in a few sentences (definitions in his/her own words, the solution to a problem or a short summary of yesterday's or this week's content). Their activity will give you several minutes to handle administrative or "class keeping" chores. You can

collect the papers or not, as you choose. Always, however, tell students the key ideas that they should have included so they have the opportunity to verify or correct their knowledge immediately.

### Anticipatory set

Even when you have to sacrifice some beginning prime time to other functions, you should take advantage of the beginning of your class to create an *anticipatory set* in your students which will take their minds off other things and focus their attention on today's content. An anticipatory set also can hook into students' past knowledge and trigger a memory or some practice which will facilitate today's learning. In addition, students' responses may give you important diagnostic information about the knowledge or skills already possessed which are prerequisite to achievement of the new learning: their cognitive, affective, or psychomotor "entry behavior."

Students' entry behavior (what they already know or can do that will help them achieve the new learning) usually is a better indicator of speed of acquisition of the new learning than is I.Q. Consequently, entry behavior constitutes important diagnostic and predictive information for a teacher. That information often can be gathered by an anticipatory set.

For example, if we asked you to generate examples of anticipatory sets you might use if you had to teach students the five types of poetic feet, you would certainly take your mind off other things and concentrate on what you knew or could remember about poetic meter ("Let's see; there was something about iambic and dactylic."). Your answer to your question could indicate your degree of sophistication in that area and give you practice in recalling what you knew. You would also hear the answers of other people with more (or less) information than you. As a result, you would be more focused on a lesson on iambic pentameter than you would be if someone just began teaching it without first capturing your attention. In addition, we would have an idea of where we should begin your instruction.

Another example of an anticipatory set might be, "Can you explain why cucumbers and okra could legitimately be served in an all fruit salad?" Such a question would surely focus you on consideration of the critical attribute that determines whether something is a fruit or a vegetable and encourage recall of what you already knew in that area. Your answer to the question would reveal information important to a teacher in the development of the subsequent lesson.

28

A third example of developing an anticipatory set might be, "Write a sentence with a dependent clause preceding an independent clause and another sentence with the independent clause coming first. Punctuate them correctly." This activity will focus students on dependent and independent clauses and get them thinking about which sentence requires a comma. It also gives the teacher examples created by students from which the class can subsequently work, something that usually is more interesting and, therefore, more motivating than using only teacher examples. If the teacher circulates, glancing at papers in the few minutes that students are writing, diagnostic information about the level of students' knowledge is immediately available (with no papers to take home and correct—a dividend in itself!) Even if not all papers are examined, representative samples will supply valid information.

The variety of effective anticipatory sets is limited only by your creativity plus your having determined with reasonable precision the objective of today's class.

### Objective

That objective becomes the second important aspect in your utilization of prime time at the beginning of your class. Students usually will expend more effort and consequently increase their learning if they know what it is they will learn today and why it is important to them. It is seldom that what we teach has no revelance to a student's life, but frequently they do not make the connection. Consequently, in most (not all) cases you will find it facilitating to tell students today's objective and the purpose or reason for that learning.

Should you wish either the objective or its relevance or purpose to be discovered or to be a surprise, that is fine. Just be sure that when you don't tell students what they will learn, that is what you intended, rather than having the omission result from your forgetting to do it. Even worse is a teacher's being unaware of the potential learning accelerant from students' knowing today's objective and its importance to them, and as a result, not even considering whether or not to identify today's objective.

Examples of setting objective and purpose are:

"From our work today, you will know how to deal with poetry you don't understand so its meaning becomes clearer to you."

"Today we'll clear up any confusion you might have about the use of commas. It will save a great deal of time because you'll know for sure that your report is correctly punctuated without having constantly to check rules."

"Today, we'll learn about calorie intake so you can regulate your weight while eating foods you enjoy."

29

"Our practice today will make it much easier for you to express your ideas correctly in German."

"We're going to learn the classification system of plants so you'll be able to categorize correctly each one in the final exam."

"After today, you'll be able to determine when conclusions are valid and when they're not. That's a skill you'll use throughout your life."

"Today we'll learn how to compare the cost of various types of interest rates so you'll always know which will cost you the least, regardless of the advertisement."

"We'll analyze different types of propaganda so you can detect which one is being used on you."

Again, let us remind you that it is *your* decision whether or not you tell students the objective or learning outcome from their effort. At times, telling them can be the wrong thing to do. Regardless of whether you tell your students, certainly *you* should know exactly what learning outcomes you are teaching to achieve so you can ascertain, with evidence either that they have achieved and you can move on, or that they have not been achieved and you must go back and reteach.

In summary, we can take advantage of prime time at the beginning of our class by:

a. Giving students something to think about or recall if there is waiting time before class can start.

b. Using an anticipatory set that will focus students on the content to be learned. In addition, that anticipatory set can provide practice that is facilitating to the acquisition of the new learning and give diagnostic evidence of the entry behavior of the students. Remember, if after deliberation, you decide not to have an anticipatory set for a particular class, that's all right. If absence of an anticipatory set is not the result of deliberation but default, that's *not* all right.

c. After students have cleared their minds of nonrelevant things and are focused on today's class, motivation to learn and increased effectiveness in learning can be achieved by letting students know the objective and why it is important (unless you wish them to discover or be surprised).

Using prime time in these three ways should facilitate students' being ready for the information, process, skill, or activity that you have designed to help them achieve the objective. How to plan for that part of your class and how to bring off your plans effectively will be the subject of our next chapter.

# V   PROVIDING INFORMATION EFFECTIVELY

Guide for Group Discussion or Individual Study

**Objectives:**

*Participants will:*

a. Identify three principles which increase the effectiveness of giving information.

b. Organize information for a subsequent class according to these principles.

c. Generate a plan for how that information will be presented to students and identify the examples to be used.

**Anticipatory Set:**

List some principles which guide you in the process of giving information to your class.

**Input & Modeling:**

Read the chapter and/or view the videotape, "Providing Information Effectively."

**Checking for Understanding & Guided Practice:**

List three principles which increase the effectiveness of giving information.

Using the content of the next information-giving session which you will teach:

a. Specify the information essential to students' understanding. Select an organizational design (temporal, cause effect, simple to complex, relationships of categories, etc.) and organize the basic information.

b. Practice giving some of the information in simple language with unambiguous examples. (This is especially fruitful if other group members do not teach your content. If they can understand your presentation, you may be sure your students will.)

c. If possible, design a model that students can experience directly.

d. Examine the printed and visual materials you are using in your class to see if they adhere to the three principles.

**Independent Practice:** Teach your planned information session to the class. Observe carefully for student reactions which will give you feedback as to which techniques were successful and which need further modification.

# PROVIDING INFORMATION EFFECTIVELY

Information constitutes the foundation for learning and thinking. Without information we can't think, make decisions, solve problems, or be creative. Once we have adequate information, we can proceed to build concepts, develop generalizations and do higher level thinking.

There are many ways to acquire information, and *there is no one best way*. In addition to direct experience, students can utilize the valuable, vicarious experiences provided by books, films, discussions and lectures.

Writers and producers of audio-visual material provide information that has had the advantage of much time and great care in preparation and editing. Once completed, however, all adjustments must be made by teacher and/or learner to speed up, slow down, skip, reread or stop to consider. Also, the writer or film maker must prepare the information for anonymous learners, not knowing whether the examples carry meaning for a particular group of learners, whether the message is understood, or whether it needs to be expanded or requires modification.

Lectures have bad reputations. "Telling is not teaching," as the saying goes. It depends on what you tell and how you tell it. Poorly designed lectures certainly do not teach effectively. A well-designed lecture, however, can be adjusted to learners' needs in terms of examples used, pacing vocabulary, and idea density. A lecture also can be modified on the basis of signals given during the lecture by students, indicating their confusion, lack of interest, or need for additional examples, or need for the relief afforded by humor. As a result, the lecturer has the advantage of being able to adjust the message as it is being delivered: to say it in a different way, to give personalized examples, to include a humorous episode, or to increase or decrease the demands on the students who are listening.

Because so much teaching is done by lecture, this chapter will focus on that method of delivering information. Regardless of the content or message, adherence to three basic principles will enable you to give information more effectively. These same principles also apply to preparation of written or audio visual materials.

## 1. Determine Basic Information and Organize it.

First, we must determine which information is basic or essential to students' understanding of the content or process, and then separate that information from information which may be desirable but is supplementary and can be acquired later. That basic information must be organized so it becomes the scaffolding or advance organizer to which students can add more complex information. For example, in understanding the contribution of Columbus' voyage, it is basic that students know the scientific beliefs of the time, why the voyage was economically desirable, what happened before, during and after the voyage, the changes which resulted from that accomplishment, etc. That basic information needs to be organized so it constitutes a tapestry of related information rather than a patchwork of bits of information.

There is no one best way to organize information. Categories for organization may be temporal, cause-effect, or topical, such as beliefs of the times, personally characteristics of the man, dangers of the voyage, etc. The organization selected should reflect the needs and interests of the students but also should promote acquistion, comprehension, and retention of the relationships within the material or process being learned.

An example of basic information that is organized temporally is: "Energy comes from the sun. That energy is absorbed by plants and enables them to use elements from the soil to manufacture food. This process is called photosynthesis. Animals eat plants and, with oxygen from the air, are able to convert them to energy. This process is called cellular respiration." Once students have perceived the basic relationships inherent in photosynthesis and respiration, they are able to add more complex information.

All information, whether it be mathematical, scientific, technical or grammatical, should be examined for basic structure and presented to students in some organized way, so the student has the foundation of concepts and generalizations upon which to build more complex understandings.

## 2. Present Basic Information in Simplest and Clearest Form.

Once we have determined the information basic to students' understanding, and then organized it so students see the relationship of the parts to each other and to the whole, we need to present that information in the simplest, clearest, and most understandable form. We should use words which we are sure the students understand and accompany concepts and generalizations with examples that are unambiguous and which highlight the essence of the information being presented. For example, in describing Columbus' sailors' fear of falling off the edge of the earth, the teacher might use the example, "Suppose you were driving a car with no brakes and you suspected a bridge over a high gorge might be washed out. You are going downhill when you round the bend to cross that bridge. How might you feel?" or "Suppose someone blindfolded you, put you on a flat roof and told you to walk a straight line along the edge. How would you feel? That's the way most of Columbus' sailors probably felt at night when they couldn't see whether they were coming to the edge of the world."

Exceptions exist to almost every generalization. While it may be appropriate to state to your students "This is not always the case," it is wise to introduce only exemplars at the beginning of instruction. Leave exceptions for a later time and introduce them only after students understand the concept, generalization, or process in its simplest form.

Examples:

"Plants must have light, water, and chemicals in order to manufacture food. Animals must have animal or plant food, water, and air in order to manufacture energy."

"Suppose you and a plant were in a beautiful sunny garden with an automatic sprinkling system. The plant would thrive, you would get hungrier and hungrier, and, if there were no plants you could eat, eventually you would die. Suppose on the other hand, you and the plant, without its roots in soil, were in a sunny, well-stocked kitchen. You would thrive; the plant would die."

At this point, don't introduce plants that are parasites and therefore do not manufacture their food.

The science of the art of citing examples is so important in teaching that the chapter, "Make Material Meaningful," will assist you to develop skill in selecting and utilizing examples that increase your students' learning and retaining the information or processes you teach.

### 3. Model the Information or Process.

Finally, if at all possible, we need to model what we mean by demonstrating a process or showing a product that elicits from the students, "Oh, I see!" or "I see what that means." Modeling is so important to learning that it is the subject of an entire chapter in this book, "Modeling What You Mean."

If the student has already experienced and can image (visualize in his/her mind) the concept or generalization being taught, a model (something tangible you can perceive in the classroom) may not be necessary. It would be silly to blindfold students and have them walk near the edge of something high. They already have experienced that feeling and can remember it. With photosynthesis it might make the concept more vivid if students perceived the growth of four plants, one without elements from the soil, another without water, a third without light, and a fourth with all three of the elements necessary for photosynthesis to occur.

Make sure, however, that your model and your examples are unambiguous and that they demonstrate vividly and validly the principle or process you are teaching. (Use an air plant or a parasite only after students understand photosynthesis and are ready for "exceptions.")

Let's see if we have practiced what we are preaching about giving information. Our advance organizer was, *whenever information is being given, whether it be by lecture or prepared materials, you need to keep three basic principles in mind:* 1) information that is basic to students' understanding must be identified and organized so that it constitutes a scaffolding or advance organizer to enable students to see the relationship of each part to other parts and to the whole, 2) information must be presented in language which is clear and unambiguous to the students, with examples which highlight the essence of the concept or generalization, and 3) *if appropriate,* a tangible model should be used so students can directly perceive the process or product.

We also attempted to explain (in simple language) what was meant by each of those three principles (using verbal examples).

Finally, we hope that what you are reading serves as a model of the process of giving information which we are attempting to convey to you.

Each of these *Mastery Teaching* chapters and videotapes was developed to constitute a model of giving written, auditory, and visual information (note, we say a model of, *not* THE WAY). As you view the videotapes that accompany each chapter, we hope you will "see" what we mean. When the academic content area you see is not your own, we hope our advance organizer with input in comprehensible language enables you to translate basic information to your own content and helps you to incorporate those techniques in your daily teaching.

# VI    TEACHING TO BOTH HALVES OF THE BRAIN

Guide for Group Discussion or Individual Study

**Objectives:**  *Participants will:*
a. Recall four principles of chalkboard use.
b. Examine prepared visuals to determine if they should be augmented by chalkboard use.
c. Design chalkboard use which demonstrates in space the relationship of ideas or concepts for subsequent classes.

**Anticipatory Set:**  List some principles which should guide a teacher's use of the chalkboard.

**Input & Modeling:**  Read the chapter and/or view the videotape, "Teaching to Both Halves of the Brain."

**Checking for Understanding & Guided Practice:**  List four principles of chalkboard use. Identify a concept or relationship in your own content and design a way you could demonstrate that relationship on a chalkboard.

Examine prepared visuals you commonly use and determine whether introducing them with a simple chalkboard diagram would facilitate students' understanding.

**Independent Practice:**  Try these instructional techniques in your next class.

# TEACHING TO BOTH HALVES OF THE BRAIN

Do you believe a picture is worth a thousand words? If your answer is "yes," you're right—*part* of the time. If your answer is "no," you're also right—*part* of the time. Then which do you use, words or pictures? *Most* of the time you need to use both so the student has an opportunity to do integrated brain processing of information.

Recent brain research has revealed that most people process information sequentially in their left hemispheres. You are probably using your left hemisphere as you read these words. You add what you're now reading to what you just read. You also will carry those ideas forward into what you read in the next paragraph. You are building "bridges" of understanding sequentially across time. Your left hemisphere is a temporal, analytical, if-then, sequential processor.

You would be using your right hemisphere if you could see my posture, facial expression, my pauses to think, and my general demeanor as I write. If you were listening to me speak, you would also use your right hemisphere to process additional information from my body language, the tone, emphasis, juncture of my speech, and from any visuals I might use to illustrate meaning. With your right hemisphere, you could "see" what I meant. It is no accident that we use the expression, "I see what you mean," or "Oh, I see!" or "In my mind's eye." The right hemisphere is the "mind's eye," and it processes information that is perceived simultaneously, where meaning is derived from visuals, non-language sound, or position and relationships in space.

Your right and left hemispheres are connected by a heavy band of nerve fibers, the corpus callosum, which enables those hemispheres to work together, to "cross talk." Neither hemisphere is the more powerful. You need them both. In the same way that you will catch more balls if you use both hands, you will catch more ideas and information if you use both hemispheres. Consequently, in teaching, we need to beam information to both hemispheres so that a student is not restricted to only right or left hemispheric input but achieves "integrated brained" learning (thereby eliminating much "lame brained" learning).

Although the evidence to support integrated hemispheric processing is relatively recent, teachers have realized the value of chalkboards since the beginning of time. But, because teachers didn't know the reason visuals were important to learning and how visual information was processed, chalkboards often were not used effectively. In addition, now that complex visual aides have become available, they also are used without discrimination with the illusion that "the more real, the better."

Figuratively speaking, we sometimes made the error of bringing an elephant into the classroom to teach the concept "gray" and wondered why everyone was distracted.

Clearly what is needed is not only an awareness of right hemispheric processing but also a set of discriminators which will help a teacher determine the conditions under which the simplicity of a chalkboard is effective and conditions when more complex visuals are indicated.

One guiding generalization is: *At the beginning of learning, present information in its simplest form.* This would indicate that the simplicity of the chalkboard should be used initially to present many concepts and ideas. However, there is more to using a chalkboard than knowing this simple generalization. When we use a chalkboard, we need to keep four basic principles in mind:

### 1. Say before writing.

The first principle is based on three assumptions: 1) We can say something faster than we can write it. Consequently, when we say it, the learner can immediately begin processing the information in his/her left hemisphere and does not have to wait until meaning begins to emerge from the words being written. 2) The learner does not have to "guess" the meaning, possibly erroneously, as (s)he tries to complete the not-yet-finished message while it is being written. 3) The silence during the time the message is being written on the chalkboard provides the 3-8 seconds neurologically necessary from initial perception of the words or message to storage of that information in short term memory. When one message or idea is followed immediately by another, it is possible for the second idea to eradicate the first. A few seconds of silence enables the learner to store a message in the "short term memory bank" for later retrieval.

Consequently, most (not all!) of the time we say what we are going to write on the chalkboard before writing it. Obviously, if for some reason we wish the learner to see an unknown message emerge or attempt to guess the complete message as it appears, we will write without stating what we are going to write.

### 2. Use key words — simple diagrams.

It is important that the learner focus on the key concepts or central ideas of what is being presented. While we may elaborate on these concepts or ideas in speech, on the chalkboard those ideas should stand out and not be lost in clutter. Consequently, we write as few words as possible. If we use a diagram, we make it simple. By doing so, we make it possible for the student's right hemisphere to process what is seen while the left hemisphere processes the elaboration provided by our words. The integration of those two functions should contribute to more effective learning and retention. For example, while we say, "On your chalkboard, use key words and simple diagrams," we will write "key words—simple diagrams."

### 3. Position = relationship.

The chalkboard provides the opportunity to indicate relationships of concepts and ideas through their position in space, a relationship which can be processed in the student's right hemisphere. An outline is an excellent example of position in space indicating relationships. Look at the following outline:

I  Techniques in Teaching
    A. Use of chalkboard
    B.  Use of complex visuals

The position of A and B indicate they are parallel ideas, both of which are subsets of, but not as inclusive or important as Roman numeral I. The position in space of the items in an outline provides an important visual input to help clarify the relationship of ideas.

If, on our chalkboard we write:

Washington
Jefferson

we imply that Washington comes first in some order (election, to be studied, discussed, etc.)

If we write:

Washington      Jefferson

we imply there is parallel or oppositional relationship, not (unless we number them) a first, second relationship. Arrows, lines, simple diagrams also indicate (to the right hemisphere) the relationship of the items on the chalkboard.

When we are aware of the power of position in space to suggest relationships, we avoid placing items on the chalkboard in a haphazard fashion or where there happens to be space. We place each item deliberately so its position indicates its relationship to other material on the chalkboard (causal, oppositional, numerical, comparative, categorical, etc.).

### 4. Erase before new concept.

In the same way that a clear head encourages clear thinking, a clean board encourages effective learning; so the final principle that guides chalkboard use is to erase everything that is not necessary before

41

proceeding to the next idea. Erasing "holes" in what is already on the chalkboard so something else can be added, erasing which leaves bits and pieces of previous ideas, writing between other ideas, utilizing every inch of space, all constitute "right hemispheric atrocities" because what you are presenting gets lost in the visual competition for attention.

Sometimes, teachers do not erase because they do not want to waste the time necessary to clean a board. They are wise to realize that each precious minute should be spent on learning. However, a simple solution to that dilemma is to give the students something to think about or to do while you are erasing.

Examples are:
1. "Be ready to tell me the four principles of chalkboard use."
2. "Make up a word problem that would require you use this process."
3. "Be ready to state in one sentence what you consider to be an important facet of Washington's personality."
4. "Say to yourself, your own definition of _____."

This technique will, 1) stimulate the student to review what has been learned, 2) hold him/her accountable for evidence of that learning, and 3) give you time to clean the board so the next idea is just as clear visually as it is in your verbal presentation.

There are times, of course, when the simplicity of the chalkboard is not as effective as is the motivational impact or the time saved by use of prepared visuals. Neither chalkboard nor prepared visuals are "good" in and of themselves; it's how they are used and for what purpose that determines their effectiveness. It is the prerogative of the teacher to decide whether the simplicity of basic information presented verbally and accompanied by simple visuals on a chalkboard will better promote learning, or whether the vividness, accuracy, and reality provided by realia, pictures, tapes, and motion pictures will be more motivating and enabling to successful learning.

Clearly, the decision is yours. Remember, however, when you use the ubiquitous chalkboard, your use should reflect awareness of the following principles:
1. Say before writing.
2. Use key words and simple diagrams.
3. Position=relationship.
4. Erase before new concept.

Your left brained, right brained, no-longer-lame brained learners will profit.

# VII  MODELING WHAT YOU MEAN

Guide for Group Discussion or Individual Study

**Objectives:**

*Participants will:*
a. State four characteristics of an effective model.
b. Develop models in their own content area which display those characteristics.
c. Incorporate models in subsequent instruction.

**Anticipatory Set:**

a. Explain the difference between a model and an example.
b. What characteristics make a model effective?

**Input & Modeling:**

Read the chapter and/or view the videotape, "Modeling What You Mean."

**Guided Practice:**

a. Identify the four characteristics of an effective model.
b. Examine models used in your classroom to see if they possess those characteristics.
c. Devise new models which will augment or improve on those used in the past.
d. Share your models with other participants for their analysis.

**Independent Practice:**

Continue to develop and analyze models used in subsequent classes and devise ways of improving them.

# MODELING WHAT YOU MEAN

"Give me an example" is a common request when we are not sure we understand what is meant. A model is one kind of example, one which a student can perceive directly in the classroom rather than having to rely on memory of some previous learning or experience. A model may be concrete, such as a model of the human heart or a model of a miniature city. A model may be a replication such as a picture, or symbolic such as a diagram or map. Or a model may be verbal, written, or spoken, such as a paragraph, sonnet, or alliteration.

"Oh, I see," or "I see what you mean" usually indicates the learner has processed a perception and assigned significance which is deeper than just the perception. For example, a teacher might see students looking out the window, doodling, yawning, slumped in their seats. The assigning of significance to that perception is indicated by "I see you think this isn't important, so let me show you with some examples how this influences your life."

Seeing, hearing, or feeling a model of "what is meant" can become a tremendous assist to understanding. "I see (or hear, or feel, or taste, or smell) what you mean" can result if the models used by the teacher have four important characteristics.

## 1. Effective models highlight the critical attribute.

One characteristic of an effective model is that it highlights (and the teacher labels) the critical attribute that distinguishes what it is, from other similar things. Unless that critical attribute is obvious, identified, and labeled, students' attention can be attracted to or distracted by non-relevant characteristics resulting in uncertainty or confusion.

Consequently, it is important that a model be carefully chosen to make sure it presents the concept or generalizations in an unambiguous way. Generating a model while teaching can be a burst of brilliance, but more often the spontaneous model is not as clear as it could be and results in confusion. Usually models should be developed or selected in advance. (Thinking on your seat is easier than thinking on your feet). "Peter Piper picked a peck of pickled peppers" is a more obvious model of alliteration than "The plowsman homeward plods his weary way." A cow is a better model of a mammal than is a whale.

Working first with a simple model of the heart with the chambers, valves, arteries, and veins clearly identifiable makes later identification of those same parts in a real heart more easily achieved.

### 2. Models avoid controversial issues.

In selecting a model, it is wise to avoid controversial issues where the emotions aroused can divert learners' attention from what is being taught. Current political issues may make interest-arousing models. They can, however, distract the learner's attention from the critical attribute of the model and center the focus on the pros and cons of an issue.

Example:

Model of the use of *is being*.

"The licensing of younger drivers is being considered" vs. "The licensing of prostitutes is being considered."

Model of the use of *its* vs. their.

"Each party considers its platform to be the best" vs. "The Democratic Party considers its platform to be the best."

### 3. First models must be accurate and unambiguous.

The beginning phase of any learning is critical to successful achievement. Errors introduced in this "prime time" are more difficult to eradicate than are errors which occur later in the learning sequence. Consequently, the first models must be accurate, something that is not as likely if models are generated by students. A well-thought-out model will present the concept as clearly as possible. Later, students can generate models to demonstrate they understand and can apply what is being learned.

### 4. Models eventually introduce nonexemplars.

Half of knowing what something is, is knowing what it is not. After you have presented several carefully selected, unambiguous models without emotional overtones and your students have demonstrated understanding, you may wish to present models which require students to make discriminations based on the presence or absence of the critical attributes which have been learned. The decision to introduce more ambiguous models is based on your judgment that students are ready for more complex discriminations and no longer need models which clearly highlight the critical attribute.

In selecting teaching segments for the videotapes in this *Mastery Teaching* series, we have tried to practice what we preached. We have shown models of teaching which emphasized the technique being discussed, that avoided controversial issues, and that were as clear as possible. We also introduced exemplars and nonexemplars of many techniques.

Sometimes it's not possible to provide a visual or verbal model which students can experience in the classroom. In that case, we encourage students to "reach into their memory banks of knowledge and experience" to supply meaning for the current learning. In the next chapter, we'll discuss the use of that technique to "make material meaningful."

# VIII   MAKING MATERIAL MEANINGFUL

Guide for Group Discussion or Individual Study

**Objectives:**

*Participants will:*
a. State six characteristics of an effective example.
b. Using the content of a subsequent class, generate examples which embody those six characteristics.
c. Design a mnemonic device to be used with content that previously has presented problems.

**Anticipatory Set:**

What principles should guide a teacher's choice of examples?

What are some problems that examples can present?

When should mnemonic devices be used?

**Input & Modeling:**

Read the chapter and/or view the videotape, "Making Material Meaningful."

**Checking Understanding & Guided Practice:**

List six principles which guide the choice of examples.

Using the content of your next class, generate examples which incorporate those principles.

Generate a mnemonic device to help students remember content which in the past has proved to be difficult.

**Independent Practice:**

Try these instructional techniques in your next class.

# MAKING MATERIAL MEANINGFUL

Meaning is one of the most important propellants of learning. Meaning, however, does not exist in material but in the relationship of that material to students' past knowledge and experience.

In the chapter, "Modeling What You Mean," you learned to generate meaning for students by using models. Models are examples that the student can directly perceive in the classroom.

We could create a *model* of the relationship of present learning to past experience and to future learning by presenting this diagram:

| Past knowledge and experience | → | Present learning to be acquired | → | Future situations to which learning is to be transferred. |

The student can perceive in visual space the relationship of past, present, and future learning.

While it is possible to provide models of speech, actions, excellent paragraphs, diagrams of interactions, or physical models of reality, often it isn't possible for students to perceive directly many of the complex concepts and generalizations we teach. Consequently, we need to become skilled in the use of two additional techniques that make material meaningful.

## A. Use of examples from students' past experience

We increase the meaning of material when we use an example from students' past experience. Such an example stimulates students to reach back into their "memory banks" and bring previous knowledge or experience forward to accelerate acquisition of new learning and to make that learning more meaningful.

The words we use in examples convey meaning only to the extent that they elicit from learners' past experience the concepts that are relevant to the present situation. For example, to a child the word *balloon* elicits the concept of a plaything or something you have at a party or carnival. To a balloonist, the same word elicits a very different concept. Using examples of sentences with those words, "We use colorful balloons at children's parties" or *"Around the World in Eighty Days is* the story of a balloon flight," clarifies which meaning is intended and brings previous learning forward to increase accuracy of meaning and accelerate acquistion of new learning.

To use examples successfully, we need to follow six basic principles:

### 1. Identify the critical attributes(s) of the present learning.

What is the attribute that is invariant whenever this concept is encountered?

Example:

In foreign languages, one critical attribute of modifiers is that they agree in plurality with the nouns they modify.

### 2. Select from students' own lives some previous knowledge or experience that exemplifies the same critical attribute.

Students' past knowledge of the use of "this and that" can be brought forward to, a) accelerate learning of agreement between nouns and modifiers and b) increase the probability of correspondence between singular and plural nouns and adjectives in the future.

Example:

This book, these books, that boy, those boys.

It is critical that the teacher select the example so it, 1) contains the same attribute, 2) is valid, and 3) has no confusing or irrelevant elements. Seldom can such examples be generated on the spot; they take a lot of thought and testing. Consequently, at initial presentation we should not ask students to supply examples. If we do, we are taking the chance of introducing confusion or irrelevancies at the beginning of learning which, as you know, is prime time for learning and remembering both errors and correct responses.

### 3. Check your example for distractors.

In an attempt to make learning interesting, it is possible to introduce distractors. "Don't bring an elephant into the classroom to teach the concept gray" is an important admonition. Notice your own reaction to "this rapist, those rapists" or "this communist, those communists" vs. the more neutral example of "this book, these books."

Students' attention can be diverted from the critical attribute being identified, and they may become focused on feelings elicited by the example. At times we may wish to imbue a learning with emotional overtones; however, most of the time emotions (with the exception of interest) can divert students' attention from the critical attribute which the example was designed to teach.

To teach a political concept by introducing it through a current "hot" situation could stir up "for'ers and agin'ers." Those emotions can distract from the concept being taught. For example, introducing the notion of legalized marijuana or legalized prostitution could distract a student's attention from learning the discriminators which separate legal from nonlegal actions. It is better to use examples such as "lobbying" or "cold medicines" which do not have such emotional overtones.

### 4. Present the example.

The teacher presents a well-thought-out example in simple and unambiguous language.

"Think of the way you use *this* and *these* to modify singular and plural nouns: "this book', 'these books.' You use *that* for the singular 'that boy' and the modifier *those* for the plural 'those boys'." In English we don't do that with all modifiers, but in foreign languages, adjectives are made singular or plural to match the nouns they modify. We say 'casa blanca' and 'casas blancas'."

### 5. Label the critical attributes or elements in the example.

You should know the students have perceived those discriminators rather than attention being focused on some irrelevant element.

Example:

"Notice that *casa* is singular, one house, so *blanca* is singular. The word *casas* is plural, more than one house, so the modifier *blancas* also must be plural. In the same way we say 'sombrero rojo' and 'sombreros rojos.'"

### 6. Present exceptions.

Finally, after students have a well-developed understanding of the concept, if there are exceptions, present them so students know the limits of the generalization they have learned.

Example:

In English, *hair* is a singular noun, but in Italian it is plural so it needs a plural modifier.

In this book, we are attempting to use examples that will "hook" into your own past teaching experience so you will bring additional meaning to the generalizations we present. This should enable you to learn pedagogical principles faster, remember them longer and transfer them more readily into your future teaching.

If teaching science is part of your past experience, seeing science examples on the *Mastery Teaching Videotapes* should connect these examples with your previous knowledge. We hope the same connections will occur if your past experience is in English, foreign language, philosophy, or physical activity. We also hope that if none of those content areas is yours, our examples are clear enough that you can extrapolate from them to your own content.

Our identifying, labeling, and demonstrating basic principles of learning should "hook" into your past teaching experiences so you bring that knowledge forward to accelerate achievement of increased teaching effectiveness.

### B. Use mnemonics.

Sometimes it is not possible to identify any past experience of students which might facilitate current learning. It is difficult to make classification systems, tables, and lists meaningful so they can easily be learned and remembered. Consequently, we need to invent artificial meaning to associate with the material. "Every good boy does fine" helps us remember the musical notes "e.g.b.d.f." We call this artificial meaning a *mnemonic device.*

Examples:

"It ads" for iamb, troque, anapest, dactyl, spandi in poetic feet.

"Dessert makes you bigger in the middle. The word *dessert* is bigger in the middle than the word *desert*. It has more s's than *desert.*"

"A princi**pal** should be your pal so the word ends that way."

"Thirty days hath September, April, June, and November. All the rest have 31, except February."

"Yours is not to reason why; just invert and multiply."

"*Latitude* is like *lateral* or sideways, horizontal rings around the earth. There's an **at** in *latitude*, like your belt is **at** your middle."

"*Longitude* has *long* in it and goes from the top to bottom of the earth. It has a 'g' in it which has a tail below the line and points to the bottom of a map and a 't' in it which points to the top so you can remember longitude goes from the top or North Pole to the bottom or South Pole.

When your students experience difficulty remembering something and you can't build in enough meaning, encourage them to create their own mnemonic, or develop several mnemonics so each student can choose the one which is most vivid and meaningful.

Obviously, when we can introduce real meaning in a concept, we will not distract the student with the creation of mnemonic devices. When real meaning is not available, however, mnemonics can assist learning.

In summary, when we can't use a model to give students the advantage of directly perceiving a concept or generalization in the classroom, we can provide vicarious experience to make material meaningful. We do this by, 1) citing an example from the students' own lives that clearly illustrates the critical attribute of the new learning and is free of distractors and emotional overtones, and 2) labeling that critical attribute in both the old and new learning to highlight the similarity between the two.

When it is not possible to use meaning from students' past experience to assist in learning and remembering lists, classification systems, or labels, we can create artificial meaning by the use of a mnemonic device.

Making material meaningful will return large dividends not only in terms of students' accelerated learning but also their retention of the material. Those two learning dividends are limited only by your ingenuity and creativity as you **make your own material meaningful** to students.

# IX CHECKING STUDENTS' UNDERSTANDING

Guide for Group Discussion or Individual Study

**Objectives:**

*Participants will:*
a. Identify techniques for checking students' understanding while teaching.
b. Generate techniques that can be used in subsequent class sessions.
c. Try out techniques to determine which contribute most to teachers' diagnostic information and students' understanding.

**Anticipatory Set:** List some techniques you use to check your students' understanding while you are teaching.

**Input & Modeling:** Read the chapter and/or view the videotape, "Checking Students' Understanding."

**Checking Understanding & Guided Practice:** Identify three techniques which check students' understanding without the necessity of correcting tests or papers.

Check your original list to see if you have been using all three techniques. Develop examples of any omitted techniques which you could use in subsequent classes.

Exchange techniques with other participants.

**Independent Practice:** Experiment with techniques for checking your students' understanding in subsequent classes and determine those which are the most effective.

# CHECKING STUDENTS' UNDERSTANDING

To say that you have taught when students haven't learned is to say you have sold when no one has bought. But how can you know that students have learned without spending hours correcting tests and papers?

We believe the job of the teacher is to *in*spire, not *per*spire. In this chapter, you'll learn three ways to check students' understanding *while* you are teaching (not at 10 o'clock at night when you're correcting papers) so you don't move on with unlearned material that can accumulate like a snowball and eventually engulf the student in confusion and dispair. Likewise, you can avoid investing additional, precious class time once the students have acquired the necessary understanding or skill.

In attempting to check understanding while teaching, teachers may commit three common errors. The most common is a teacher's ubiquitous, "O.K.?" with assumption that student silence means it is O.K. and they understand. "We've finished this chapter, O.K.?" "Let's move on to the next section, O.K.?" What student is going to be brave (or brash) enough to say, "No, it's not O.K. You're going too fast!"

A second common (and not very effective) way to check students' understanding is a statement, "You all understand, don't you? You don't have any questions, do you?" Few students are willing to admit publicly they don't understand. In fact, most students work hard to keep their teacher from discovering that they don't know or can't do. Yet one of the most important pieces of information teachers can have is the knowledge that students have not yet acquired the necessary understanding.

A third frequently used but not very useful method for checking students' understanding is the query, "Now, does anyone have a question?" Too often such a query carries the implication that "If you do have questions, you obviously weren't listening or you're not very bright." Such a query can also be an invitation for students to divert teachers by asking for unneeded information ("Do we have to type it?"). Sometimes students think the teacher wishes questions and, even though no information is needed, they try to oblige. Students also may be employing a delaying tactic to avoid getting to work or moving on to new content.

All three of these dysfunctional methods for checking students' understanding can result in a teacher's proceeding, blissfully unaware that students are lost. This problem can be prevented (and hours of correction of papers saved) by employing any one or a combination of the following techniques.

## 1. Signaled Answers

A simple way to check understanding is to pose a question or statement and have every student signal the answer.

Examples:

"Look at the first multiple choice question. Decide which answer you would select and when I say 'show me', place that number of fingers under your chin. (Peripheral vision doesn't help students copy their neighbor's selection). If plagiarism occurs, you can direct students to "close your eyes; now show me." Using this techniques makes it easy to detect the student who needs a visual assist from his peers.

"Thumbs up if the statement I make is true, down if false, to the side if you're not sure." Encouraging students to reveal their confusion so it can be cleared up then and there will bring rich dividends in later test performance.

"Make a plus with your fingers if you agree with this statement, a minus if you don't, and a zero if you have strong feelings."

"Show me with your fingers if sentence 1 or sentence 2 has a dependent clause."

"Raise your hand each time you hear (or see) an example of _____."

Occasionally, some teachers feel that this is "baby stuff" and students will feel silly or resent this type of classroom probing of their understanding. It has been the experience of teachers and university professors who have employed these techniques, *after* explaining that they are providing students the opportunity to check their own understanding so that misconceptions can be cleared up immediately rather than being revealed on a test, that students respond enthusiastically. When signaled answers are accompanied by an explanation of the reason why a certain response is correct, students can, without penalty, correct misunderstandings and learn to apply the generalization to new questions or situations.

## 2. Choral responses

A second way of checking students' understanding is to ask the group a question and get choral response. ("Is this an example of dactylic or iambic?") The strength as well as the correctness of the response can give valuable clues as to whether most students know the answer.

Choral responses, however, have two problems. One is that some students don't answer. As a result, the teacher doesn't know if those students know the answer but are covert learners (respond within themselves but not out loud) or whether they don't know the answer. The second problem with choral responses is that some of the students who do respond may be "coat tailing" (making their mouths move just as you do in the second chorus of the national anthem even though you don't really know all the words). Teaching dividends from choral responses are greater than testing dividends.

In spite of these two problems, choral responses have value. They alert the teacher to the strength of students' correct responses. Choral responses are also an excellent way for a student who doesn't know the answer to learn the correct response without visibility or humiliation.

### 3. Sample individual response.

A third technique for checking understanding is for the teacher to beam a question to the whole class. ("Be ready to give me an example of this generalization."). Then call on individual students and make an inference on the basis of the stratum of the class each student represents. If a bright student is confused, a justifiable inference is that most of the students don't understand. If an average student doesn't know, the inference is that a substantial portion of the class needs to spend more time on the subject. If a slower students responds correctly, the class probably is ready to move on.

The question arises of what to do when only a few students remain confused. If this occurs early in the teaching of a new content, it is justifiable to spend some more time on that content. The result may be "overlearning" by the rest of the students, but as long as examples are new (rather than the teacher's contributing to boredom by repeating the same thing) retention of the material will be increased for all students.

If considerable time has been spent on the content and there still remains a small group who haven't achieved the learning, it is better to plan a remedial session for those students while the rest of the class is engaged in something else or when they are not present.

Another way of sampling individual responses is to pose a question and require students to write a *brief response*. While they are writing, the teacher can circulate among the students to see if the majority have achieved the learning or there is still much confusion. The teacher also can select students' vivid or clarifying written responses to be presented to the total class. This will add variety and increase everyone's understanding of the concept, discrimination, or generalization being presented.

## Tests, Papers, or Observations of Performance

Eventually, students must demonstrate their achievement of learning by producing a product that validates that achievement. Usually this is a test, paper, or performance. Teachers need to be alert, however, to the fact that some students have a facility for "running off at the pen" and sounding brilliant even though they may not understand. Unless a ponderous research paper is the objective, it is wise to limit the amount of writing permitted. One sentence, one paragraph or, a one-page answer requires very clear understanding rather than fuzzy rambling. It also gives the teacher less to correct and leaves no question as to the student's comprehension. In addition, it sets a premium on quality rather than quantity, a highly desirable intellectual goal.

Short papers (1-5 pgs.) enable you to return them promptly so students have immediate feedback as to what they have achieved and what they still need to learn. Teacher comments written on those papers are essential if students are to have specific knowledge of what they know and what they need to learn. Grades simply tell a student the paper was acceptable or unacceptable but not *why* or what needs to be added or changed. For learning that can be measured only by direct observation of performance (athletics, music, arts, teaching), that performance becomes the test to be evaluated. The criteria for performance need to be made explicit so feedback can be specific.

In summary, we are suggesting that you check your students' understanding by, 1) signals, 2) choral or short written responses, 3) samples of students' individual responses, and eventually tests, papers, or demonstration of the target learning.

You will be amazed by how such "dip sticking" *while* you are teaching will contribute to your knowledge of what has been learned and what needs to be retaught. The result in subsequent tests, papers, and performance will be increased achievement.

# X  PRACTICE DOESN'T MAKE PERFECT

Designing Effective Practice

Guide for Group Discussion or Individual Study

**Objectives:**
*Participants will:*
a. State and answer the four questions related to practice.
b. Design teaching plans which incorporate principles of practice in subsequent classes.

**Anticipatory Set:**
List some factors which you think should be incorporated in students' practice to produce the most improvement in cognitive, affective, or psycho-motor performance.

**Input & Modeling:**
Read the chapter and/or view the videotape, "Practice Doesn't Make Perfect."

**Checking for Understanding & Guided Practice:**
List the four questions about practice and their answers.

Classify your original list in terms of the four answers.

Identify learnings which have been difficult for your students and then design ways of incorporating the four principles of practice in your class sessions.

Discuss the conditions under which class time should be used for practice and those conditions when practice should be done outside of class.

**Independent Practice:**
Try these teaching techniques in subsequent classes and determine which are most effective.

# PRACTICE DOESN'T MAKE PERFECT
# DESIGNING EFFECTIVE PRACTICE

Practice, "doing it again," does not make perfect. Witness the freeway drivers who "do it again" every day but don't improve. You know someone to whose house you dread going for dinner. That person has been practicing cooking for years but still can't get it all together.

If one automatically improved with practice, all older teachers would be better than younger ones, and we know that is not the case.

In order for practice to improve performance, whether it be basketball, physics, writing, math, vocational education, or teaching, that practice must be designed and conducted according to four psychological principles. These principles are the answers to four questions you must ask when you design practice for your students.

In this chapter, you will learn to ask and answer those four critical questions so students' practice increases their learning and improves their performance.

*Question 1:* *How much material should be practiced at one time?*
*Answer:* *A short meaningful amount.* Always use meaning (not mathematics!) to divide your content into parts.

Introduce a short meaningful "chunk" to your students. Then give several examples or go over it again in a different way. Make sure you check their understanding and their reasonable accomplishment before you move on. (See Chapter 9, "Checking Students' Understanding.") If you explain to your students that you're focusing on a short meaningful amount and why you're doing it, you'll encourage them to apply those same techniques when they're practicing independently.

Examples:

Practice the identification of dependent and independent clauses. When that has been achieved by most of the students, practice the use of the comma in sentences that begin with dependent clauses.

Practice the use of the apostrophe in contractions. Only after that has been learned, practice the use of the apostrophe in possessives.

Practice learning the critical attributes of algae. Only after they have been learned, move on to fungi.

Practice identification of the setting of a story. Only after that has been reasonably accomplished, move on to plot.

Practice with regular verbs. Only after they are learned, move to irregular.

Practice only one part of a performance. When that has been reasonably (not perfectly) learned, move to the next part. While you may introduce the "total" to show where the part to be practiced belongs, students' practice should be focused on a short meaningful part.

*Question 2:   How long in time should a practice period be?*
*Answer:       A short time so the student exerts intense effort and has an intent to learn.*

Key words in the answer to that question are *intent* to learn and *intense* or highly motivated effort on the part of the student. Consequently, because focus and intensity are not easily sustained, the practice period on any one aspect of learning should be short. Several short, highly motivated practice periods will yield more improvement than a long one which often deteriorates into lessening of effort and distraction. Unfortunately, much practice is done with the motivation to "get it over with" rather than to "get it learned." We, as teachers, contribute to this when we acknowledge or reward "finishing" or "completion" rather than "learning" or quality performance. Rather than asking, "Have you finished it?" we should ask "Have you learned it?" Obviously, the more complex the task, the longer is the time needed to practice. Even then, short, intense practice periods yield the greatest learning dividends.

Often a practice period should be broken into segments practicing different things rather than practicing one thing for the total period.

Examples:

Spend ten minutes practicing dependent clauses; then ten minutes practicing possessives. Go back to check dependent clauses, then move on to descriptive words. Go back to check apostrophes with descriptive phrases. Finally, put them all together. "Although the insufferable man's language offended us, we managed to sustain our equanimity."

Practice the critical attributes of algae. When they are reasonably learned, move on to fungi. After that is learned, check that the attributes of algae are retained, and move on to liverworts. Spend a short intense period on each and check back so students know they are accountable not only for learning but for remembering what was learned.

Short, intense practice periods are equally important for psychomotor skills, something known for a long time by music teachers and voice, drama and athletic coaches.

66

*Question 3: How often should students practice?*
*Answer:      New learning, massed practice. Older learning, distributed practice.*

There are two answers to this question depending on whether the learning is new to the student. New learning is not very durable; so several practice periods scheduled close together will yield very rapid learning. Practice periods that are close together in time are called *massed* practice. Massed practice is accomplished when you employ several different examples embodying the same principle, several questions requiring the same discrimination, several problems involving the same operation, several different situations requiring the same mode of attack. Massed practice produces rapid learning. Students utilize this principle when they "cram" for an exam. Material can be quickly learned, but it also can be quickly forgotten unless the practice schedule changes.

Once something is understood or has been learned, the practice periods need to be spaced farther and farther apart. Increasing time intervals between practice is call *distributed practice,* and it yields long remembering. We distribute practice when we periodically review previously learned material.

For the most effective use of practice time, practice should be massed at the beginning of learning. Then practice periods should be changed to a distributed schedule. Translated into your class periods, this means going over something several times when you first introduce it. If you move on to something else, come back to the new material again and review it at the end of the period. At the next class period, check to make sure the material is remembered. If it is, you don't need to review it until a few class periods later. If the material is forgotten, you will need to reteach it and review it again the next time the class meets. Homework can be an excellent opportunity to mass practice something learned today (providing it *was* learned and mistakes won't be practiced). Homework also can be used to distribute practice on previously learned material.

While a massed and then a distributed practice schedule may seem to consume a great deal of time when you could be moving on, you will find that time is saved in the long run because students remember and can use what they have learned. Explaining why you are scheduling practice in this way will help your students schedule their own practice and review periods so they not only learn faster but remember longer.

*Question 4: How will students know how well they have done?*
*Answer:       Give specific knowledge of results.*

To practice without knowledge of results usually is a waste of time. At first, the answer to the question, "How am I doing?" needs to come from the teacher who sets the criteria for excellence in performance. Once students know the criteria for an acceptable performance they can evaluate their own performance or use materials to check correctness.

Students receive knowledge of results as the teacher asks questions, has students signal responses, or write brief responses on paper, and then tells students the correct answer and the *reason why it is correct*. By doing this, students learn the criteria to be used later in evaluating their own responses.

Let's practice what we preach and mass your practice on the information in this chapter. On a sheet of paper, jot down the four questions to be asked in designing students' practice. Then in a short phrase, write the answer to each question. Finally, check your answers by reviewing the information on the previous pages.

Distribute your practice by later checking your recall of the questions and answers.

Most importantly, practice implementing these four principles of effective practice as you conduct or assign practice in your classes. Your students' accelerated learning and increased retention will be ample evidence of the success of your efforts.

# XI  GUIDING THEIR INITIAL PRACTICE

Guide for Group Discussion or Individual Study

**Objectives:**  *Participants will:*
a. Identify four ways to guide initial practice.
b. Generate examples of each of these techniques.
c. Plan for the use of these techniques in subsequent classes.

**Anticipatory Set:**  List techniques which you have found useful during students' initial practice of a new learning so errors are minimized and corrected.

**Input & Modeling:**  Read the chapter and/or view the videotape, "Guiding Their Initial Practice."

**Checking for Understanding & Guided Practice:**  List and discuss the four techniques for guiding initial practice.

Check original lists and identify those techniques which are examples of the four techniques.

Plan for use of these techniques in subsequent classes.

Share your plans with other participants.

**Independent Practice:**  In subsequent classes, determine which techniques are the most enabling for your students.

# GUIDING THEIR INITIAL PRACTICE

The difference between knowing how something should be done and being able to do it is the quantum leap in learning. The springboard for that leap is developed by *guided* initial practice accompanied by *feedback* that gives the learner information about what is correct, what needs to be improved, and *how* to improve performance.

New learning is like wet cement; it can easily be damaged. A mistake at the beginning of learning can have long lasting consequences that are hard to eradicate. The mispronounciation of a new word or an error in the way you hold a tennis racquet when you are first learning to play will take more time to remedy than it would have taken to learn correctly in the first place. Consequently, it is essential that students' beginning ventures in any new learning or skill be guided by the teacher in order to minimize the chance of errors and to provide the feedback essential to improve performance.

One usually thinks of practice as something done outside of the classroom. Once the teacher is satisfied that errors won't be practiced, this should be the case. Hours of learning time and energy can be saved, however, and achievement will reach a higher level more rapidly if students' initial practice is guided and monitored by the teacher.

Four techniques for guiding initial practice are similar to those used to check initial understanding. They are:

## 1. Guiding the group through each step in practice

It will help to eliminate initial errors if the teacher breaks practice into small steps and verbally guides the group through or models each step. "The first thing we need to determine is _____. Now we will proceed to _____. This will be followed by _____."

The teacher's stating the thinking process that influences the decisions or choices being made and then identifying what must be considered in making those decisions can lead a student through a thinking process which later must occur without guidance when the student is practicing independently. The teacher's modeling and verbal guidance also alert students to those critical points where potential for errors exists and develop the criteria for decisions or strategies to avoid those errors.

Examples:

"I'm thinking of the gender of the noun to determine the ending of its modifier."

"First, I'm going to list all the variables I can think of that might influence this interaction. Then I'm going to take each one separately and _____."

71

"I'll start with a rough generalization that will be the thesis of my paper. Then I'll briefly list all the facts that support that generalization."

It is common to break physical performance into small steps and guide the student through each step regardless of whether the performance is playing a violin, passing a football, learning a dance routine, or singing a song. It is equally effective, but not so common, to guide a student through a cognitive or affective process which, though covert, often involves those same small steps.

### 2. Monitoring Group Responses and Giving Feedback

*Choral responses:*

After the teacher has modeled the thinking process and has guided the class through each step of that process, students need to practice with immediate feedback as to whether their responses are correct or incorrect, and why. This practice can be accomplished through choral responses. If an individual is not sure or is incorrect, (s)he is not highly visible and can build in correction without public embarrassment or humiliation. This technique also gives the teacher valuable information as to what most students know and what needs additional information or clarification.

Examples:

"Everybody respond to my question. Is this an example of _____ or _____?"

"Think of the name of the poet who wrote these lines _____. Who was it?"

"What is the next step in this process?"

Usually the teacher will validate the answer and give the reason it is correct. "Yes, _____ is correct because _____."

*Signaled responses:*

A second way group responses can be monitored and feedback given is by asking students to signal responses. At first, some teachers are concerned about asking students to signal for fear the students will object to "baby stuff." When the reason for signaling is explained, "It lets me know if I have made it clear or whether we need to spend more time on it," student reluctance disappears. This technique is used effectively by teachers in both high school and university classes.

Example:

"If this statement is true, thumbs-up: false, thumbs-down. Thumbs to the side if you can't tell or aren't sure or if you wish further clarification." Knowing when students are confused or aren't sure is important information for a teacher.

Clarification, at times of confusion or uncertainty, can be built in at the moment it is needed rather than in the final paper or exam when it is too late to be of maximum benefit. Students who are timid about asking questions often can more comfortably reveal their need for clarification through signaled responses.

Students should be encouraged to give a signal for "don't understand" throughout class time. This signal alerts the teacher to any part of the lesson that is not clear or needs additional examples.

Examples:

"Decide whether 1, 2, 3, or 4 is correct and show me that number of fingers. Make a fist if you don't know."

"If a comma is needed in this sentence, make one with your finger. If none is needed, make a zero. If you're not sure, thumbs to the side."

"Close your eyes and make a plus with your fingers if what I state is true, a minus if it is false, a zero if you don't know."

"I have numbered the categories on the chalkboard. Show me with your fingers the number of the category to which this item belongs."

*Composite responses:*

A third way the group can practice is by having different members of the group contribute a part of the answer to make a composite correct response. When a teacher uses this technique, every member of the group must practice thinking through the process and following each step because any one might be called on to supply the next step. The teacher should call on students whose responses have high probability of being correct, so errors are not introduced at the initial stage of learning. Remember the job of the teacher is to help students be right, not to catch them being wrong.

Examples:

"Be ready to state a topic sentence about the problem we just discussed _____."

"While I'm writing it, get ready to state a next sentence that might come in the paragraph."

"Be ready to add another sentence."

"Think of the first thing I should do." Student responds. "Right, what do I do next?" Another student supplies answer. "What follows this?" A third student supplies answer.

### 3. Sampling group understanding through an individual's response

Often the teacher can sample the understanding of the group by calling on individuals who represent certain stratum of the group (the most able, average, least able). From the correctness of that individual's response (or the errors made) the teacher can estimate the understanding of other members of that stratum. If an able student can't do it, most of the class needs additional instruction. If a slower student is correct, the class is probably ready for independent practice.

More typical is the situation where part of the class is ready for independent practice and the rest of the class isn't. In that case the teacher might say, "If you feel you understand, make up three questions which would be a valid test of someone's understanding of this material and be ready to pose them to the class. The rest of us will work together a little bit longer."

An excellent stimulus to students' understanding material is for them to design a test of that material. Also, useful future examination questions may emerge from their efforts, thereby saving teacher time. Those students who feel confident might go ahead by themselves to finish the questions or material. They might also preview the next chapter pulling out main ideas to build the scaffolding for future group learning.

An important adjunct to group or individual practice is the feedback that lets a student know why the answer was correct, or, if incorrect, what needs to be changed.

Examples:

"That was an excellent example because _____."

"You are right to put a comma there because the dependent clause preceded the independent."

"Your word order is correct. Now make your verb match your plural subject."

"Your example is ambiguous because _____. Can you make it tighter?"

### 4. Monitoring each individual's written response

A brief, written response from each individual can be monitored as the teacher circulates through the group. In this way, individual help can be given to those who need it. Because time is limited for this type of activity, the teacher doesn't circulate randomly but selects specific students who might need help. If common errors exist, they can be quickly perceived, the class can be interrupted to correct them through additional instruction, and then students can go back to work while the teacher checks to see that the correction was effective.

Example:

"Work these problems by yourself."

"Stop and look up here. Everyone is having trouble with number four. Let's go through it together."

"Now, go ahead with the rest."

In summary, a teacher can prevent costly initial mistakes with destructive consequences by:

1. Guiding the group through each step in initial practice.
2. Monitoring choral, signaled, and composite group responses and giving students feedback.
3. Inferring understanding through the responses of sample students.
4. Monitoring individual's brief written responses.

The dividends from guided initial practice are realized in faster, more accurate, and more satisfying student performance.

# XII EXTENDING THEIR THINKING

Guide for Group Discussion or Individual Study

**Objectives:**

*Participants will:*

a. Identify six levels of cognition.

b. Explain or describe each level in their own words.

c. Generate examples in their own content at all six levels.

d. Develop plans to extend students' thinking in subsequent classes.

**Anticipatory Set:**

Which one of each of the following pairs of questions requires more complex thinking? Why?

a. What did Columbus do?

b. Who was the braver, Columbus or the first astronauts? Why?

a. Is this a restrictive or a nonrestrictive clause?

b. Use this same beginning "The man" and complete one sentence with a restrictive clause and another sentence with a non-restrictive clause.

a. Conduct the experiment outlined in the book.

b. Design an experiment to support or refute the hypothesis.

**Input & Modeling:**

Read the chapter and/or view the videotape, "Extending Students' Thinking."

**Checking for Understanding & Guided Practice:**

List the six levels of thinking.

Explain or describe each level.

Generate examples or questions and activities in your own content at each level.

Develop plans to extend students' thinking in subsequent classes.

**Independent Practice:**

Monitor your future classes to make sure assignments require thinking beyond the comprehension level.

# EXTENDING THEIR THINKING

The ability to think creatively, to solve problems, and to make satisfying and productive decisions are fundamental goals of education. In order to help students achieve those goals we need to become sensitive to, as well as learn how to elicit, higher levels of their thinking. One useful classification system of such thinking has been developed by Benjamin Bloom* who separated cognition into six levels.

## I Knowledge

Possession of information or knowledge is the foundation from which all higher thinking grows. Think about a *yik*. "A what?" you ask. A *yik*. You can't think about it because you have no knowledge or information to indicate what a *yik* is or means. To think about it, you would need to get some information either by direct experience with a *yik* or vicariously through reading, observing, talking, or listening. Making information available to our students is so important to thinking that Chapter 5, in this book, "Providing Information Effectively," has been devoted to one way of accomplishing it.

Questions from the teacher, from a text, or in a test, that check whether a student possesses information are those questions which require recall such as:

"Write the formula for_____."
"What countries did Napoleon conquer?"
"Who wrote "Ode to a Grecian Urn?"
"List the major wars in which the U.S.A. was involved."
"State the rule for making these words plural."
"Give the definition of_____."
"Solve for x: 2x + 30 = 80."

To answer each of these questions a student must recall or locate information but not necessarily understand that information.

## II Comprehension

The second level of thinking is comprehension of the information that has been recalled or located. Information is not useful unless it is understood. Suppose you received the information that a *yik* is a *zuk*. Now you can correctly answer the question, "What is a *yik*?" by "It's a *zuk*." Not comprehending, however, you don't know whether a *yik* is only

---

*Bloom, Benjamin, ed. *Taxonomy of Educational Objectives.*
*The Classification of Educational Goals. Handbook I:*
*Cognitive Domain* (New York: David McKay Co., 1956).

one form of a *zuk* or whether you ride them or eat them. This may sound like a lot of "gobbledy gook" to you, but that's the way content sounds to students when they don't really understand it. A piece of information is like a brick. It's excellent material for future building, but it only clutters up your yard unless you understand how to make use of it.

Bits of information clutter up a student's mind unless that information is understood well enough to be used to build more complex concepts and generalizations. We talk about some students in our classes having a high T.R.I. (Trivia Retention Index) because they can recall a lot of information which they don't seem to understand. Consequently, that information is not useful to them. Their lack of understanding becomes obvious when we ask them to use that information to solve a problem, draw conclusions, or create a new hypothesis.

One way we can check whether students comprehend the information they possess is to have them state that information in their own words rather than recalling what they have read or heard.

Examples:

"Say in your own words some of the things we discussed today."

"Give your own definition of *persevere*."

Answer: "To persevere means that you make yourself keep on doing something even though, at times, you would like to stop."

"Define *courage*."

Answer: "Courage means that you are afraid, but you make yourself go on as if you were not afraid."

"Define *teaching*."

Answer: "Teaching is the process of examining what is to be learned and using the science of cause-effect relationships in learning plus one's own artistry to help students achieve that learning."

An additional way we can check students' comprehension is to have them give an example of the concept or generalization being learned.

Examples:

"Give an example of a time when you persevered."

Answer: "I wanted to see Shogun on TV, but I had a paper due, so I made myself keep on writing until I finished. I persevered."

"Give me an example of courage."

Answer: "I remember one night when I was little, I heard noises and wanted to go into my parents' room, but I acted courageously. I pointed my flashlight out the window to scare the intruder and saw it was the wind blowing the tree branches against the window."

"Give me an example of a change in your teaching."

Answer: "Last year I thought my students ought to do research reports; so I told them to. This year I am teaching them each skill: locating information, taking notes, organizing their notes, writing the introduction, the body of the report and conclusions, doing the bibliography, etc. Instead of admonishing them to do reports, I now am teaching them how."

When a student comprehends information, rather than merely recalling it, that information becomes useful in future problem solving or decision making and makes creativity more probable.

## III Application

Information and skills become useful when they can be applied to a new, not previously encountered situation. Generalizations can be used to solve new problems. Previous experience can be used to predict outcomes, estimate answers, extrapolate from data, and/or avoid errors. It is important that students have experience in applying whatever they learn to new problems or situations. At the application level, most of the time we are looking for convergent thinking.

Examples:

"Using what you know about the plural form of words ending in 'y', make the following imaginary words plural: *zady, paisy.*" (Note if real words are used such as *lady, baby,* the student may not be applying the rule but merely recalling correct spelling.)

"If you wished to keep a liquid that was very similar to water from freezing, what might you add to it?"

"Make sure you apply what you have learned about organizing notes to your term paper."

"Locate the metaphors in the story."

"In what way is our class a democracy? A dictatorship?"

The ability to apply a concept or a generalization to a new situation is the launching pad for all higher level thinking. Bloom separates advanced thinking into three levels. It is not essential that you are able to identify precisely which level you are encouraging or requiring of students. What *is* important is that you make sure students have information they understand and can apply *before* you expect them to achieve successfully more complex cognitive feats.

## IV Analysis

Creative thinking and problem solving begin with analytic thinking: mentally taking something apart to understand better the relationship of the parts to each other and to the whole. Analysis may be accomplished using language, sonorous cues, or visual space. To analyze, one must be able to think categorically: that is to organize and reorganize information into categories.

Examples:

"List arguments which would support the position and arguments that could impeach it." (This assumes the rationale for the arguments can be extracted from the material and the information is not merely recalled from a previous encounter.)

"In what ways is *Hamlet* typical of Shakespeare, and in what ways is the play unique?"

"Which factors do you believe contributed most to Edison's genius?"

"On the basis of your observations, which variables could you eliminate as causal factors?"

Once students can "take information apart" the better to understand interrelationships, they are ready to reorganize that information in new patterns and create with it.

## V Synthesis

The fifth category of complexity in thinking is synthesis or invention: the creation of something which is new to its creator. One difference between application and synthesis is that usually the former is convergent but the latter results from divergent thinking: something new and different. Note, however, that a student can create only *after* (s)he has skills and information which then are applied divergently to a new situation. Creativity does not spring from a vacuum but emerges from rigor and structure. The greatest artists in performance or in thinking have spent countless hours developing comprehension and application in their discipline before the synthesis of masterpieces emerged.

All students have potential for creative thinking. In many that potential has been scientifically extinguished by their "majoring" in recalling THE right answer rather than using information as a launching pad for more complex thinking. Giving students the foundation for, and practice in, higher level thinking, plus rewarding that thinking (verbally, with extra credit, with an "A," with recognition) when it occurs will encourage its frequency.

Examples:

"Design your own experiment to demonstrate _____."

"Create a hypothesis that would explain _____."

"Write a poem or essay expressing your feelings about _____."

"Invent a new way to _____."

"Create a non-verbal statement (visual, auditory, kinesthetic, etc.) expressing _____."

## VI Evaluation

Evaluation, the making of judgments when there is no one answer which is right for everyone, is one of the most complex levels of thinking because evaluation is based on all other cognitive levels. Evaluation or judgment is essential to all intelligent and satisfying decisions.

When the criteria are known ("Identify the experiment that manipulates only one variable at a time."), the learner is simply applying those criteria to a new situation (application). If the criteria are not given ("Which research project do you consider to be better designed? Support your judgment."), the learner must examine criteria from several categories and then select those which in his/her judgment are the most relevant to the particular situation.

The learner's values (intellectual, aesthetic, social, moral) are usually reflected in cognition at the level of evaluation.

Examples:

"Which poet did you enjoy more? Why?"

"What do you believe was the person's most significant contribution? Support your answer."

"Write three introductory paragraphs. Star the one you think is best. State your reasons."

We are tempted to believe students who agree with us are good thinkers and those who disagree are not. Note that in evaluation, any judgment that can be supported is valid. Performance at the evaluation level tightens students' thinking and opens them to the consideration of different points of view: a significant goal of education.

We reiterate that the important skill for you as a teacher, is not to be able to classify the level of thinking of every assignment, but to be aware that the cognitive launching pad of knowledge and comprehension which can be applied to new situations, plus your encouragement of higher levels of thinking make it possible for students' minds to soar.

# XIII   DIGNIFYING ERRORS TO PROMOTE LEARNING

Guide for Group Discussion or Individual Study

**Objectives:**

*Participants will:*
1. Practice generating responses that, a) dignify an incorrect answer, b) prompt the correct answer, and c) hold students accountable.
2. Use these techniques in subsequent class periods.

**Anticipatory Set:**

"If you asked this question, 'Who was the first elected president of the U.S.?' and a student answered 'Lincoln,' how would you respond to that student?"

Encourage a variety of responses by, "What is another possible response?"

**Input & Modeling:**

Read the chapter and/or view the videotape, "Dignify Errors to Promote Learning."

**Checking for Understanding & Guided Practice:**

List the three steps in correcting errors.

Practice responding to incorrect answers such as:

"What is our national capital?"
   Answer: "New York."

"What is a productive response to a student's error?"
   Answer: "You're wrong!"

"Why are we looking at these videotapes?"
   Answer: "Because we have to."

Participants should recall incorrect answers they have encountered in their classes and generate a variety of teacher responses (there is no one right way) which dignify the incorrect answer, prompt the correct response, and hold the student accountable.

**Independent Practice:**

Use this teaching technique in subsequent classes until it becomes automatic.

## DIGNIFYING ERRORS TO PROMOTE LEARNING

If there is one thing in teaching that you can bet your life will happen, it's that some students will produce incorrect answers. Unfortunately, in our society a wrong answer can become a "put down." Most of us dread appearing stupid or ignorant. Frequently, students will not participate or volunteer answers in order to avoid the risk (and humiliation) of being wrong. As a result, we may not have as much student participation in our class as we desire.

In this chapter, you will learn one way to deal with an incorrect answer so the student will learn the correct response but will not feel "put down." How to do this is the *science* of effective teaching. How *you* do this is the *art* of effective teaching. If your teaching employs only science, you're a technologist. If your "art" does not have a scientific foundation, you're simply a promising amateur. You need both art and science to be a master teacher. (The Taj Mahal is not a departure from the scientific principles of physics and engineering but an artistic manifestation of those principles.)

When your student gives an incorrect answer, there isn't just one thing (s)he doesn't know; there are two. One, (s)he doesn't know the correct answer to the question. Two, (s)he doesn't know the question to which the answer given really belongs. Let's look at a very simple example: (Remember, first examples should be simple and unambiguous.) If to the question, "How much is $5 \times 7$?" the answer given is 30, the student doesn't know that $5 \times 7 = 35$ and also doesn't know that $5 \times 6 = 30$. Consequently, there are *two* things which that student needs to learn, not just one. To teach both we:

a. Dignify the student's response by supplying the question or statement to which the answer belongs. "You would be right if I had asked $5 \times 6$. $5 \times 6$ is 30. You are in the five times tables." Your comment tells the student, "You had something important to offer; you simply got it in the wrong place."

b. Next, we need to give the student an "assist" or "prompt." Remember, our function as teachers is to help students be right, *not* to catch them being wrong! An example of a prompt might be, "Suppose I ask you to buy six nickel packages of gum. That would be 30¢. If you bought one more package for yourself, one more nickel, seven 5¢ packages of gum, what would that cost?" With that assistance, usually the student will respond, "35¢."

c. Our final professional obligation is to hold that student accountable. It's important that we assist with but equally important that we insist on students' learning and remembering. Consequently, we need to convey that message of accountability to the student. "Now, so that everyone remembers the answer, let's go over it again. How much is 5 × 7? And what multiplied by 5 equals 30? I'll bet you'll remember that if I ask you the same question tomorrow." The unmistakable message is, "I expect you to!"

Holding students accountable can be *gentle*. "Let's go over that one more time so you remember it." Accountability can be *medium*. "I'll check with you tomorrow to be sure you remember." Or, the expectations we beam to students can be *unmistakable*. "You will be accountable for this on the test." The measure of accountability is determined by the needs of the student for support in performance or demand for performance (for "patting" or "pitchforking").

Frequently students do not feel accountable. "Missed it, forget it" can become their creed. We can change this attitude to "I'd better remember it," as we, a) dignify a student's incorrect response, b) prompt the correct response, and c) suggest that accountability for correct responses will be expected in future encounters with the information.

Examples:

Teacher: "Is 'although, you have been studying,' a dependent or independent clause?"

Student: "Independent."

Teacher: "If I had said, 'You have been studying' that would be an independent clause because it could be a sentence. When it is preceded by 'although,' it implies that something else is needed to finish it. It can't stand alone so it is _____. Let's try another example, so it is clear to you."

Teacher: "What is the critical attribute of an argumentative essay?"

Student: "It gives information."

Teacher: "You're right that we must give information in order to *persuade* the reader that our point of view is correct. But, if we only give information, we are writing an expository essay. What else do we intend to accomplish with our argument?"

Student: "Oh, we want to persuade the reader that our argument is correct."

Teacher: "Right, so when we only give information, we are writing what kind of essay?"_____"And when our information is for the purpose of persuading the reader that our point of view is correct, we are writing what kind of essay?"_____"Now you know the difference, and you shouldn't have any trouble with that on the exam."

Only rarely, if we think the student needs to experience failure, do we use the response of "no" ("No, $5 \times 6$ is not 35," "No, that is not an example of _____. "No, Napoleon did not _____." Watch that "no" that always wants to slip out from your lips. It can be lethal and discourage students from further participation. When you hear an incorrect response, suppress your "no's" unless you mean to use them deliberately. Most of the time you will find that you can dignify students' incorrect responses, prompt them to correct answers and hold them accountable, thereby encouraging comfortable, safe and successful participation in your class.

At times, in spite of your prompt, a student may give a second wrong answer. Again, you need to dignify the response by supplying the question or statement to which the second incorrect answer belongs. After doing so, move to a different student. (There's no point in mining for diamonds where none exist.) Then you need to determine whether to come back to the original student to let him/her know (s)he's accountable or whether to wait until later to come back privately. In either case, be sure you *do* come back so students know they're responsible for learning.

Example:

> If, after your prompt for the answer "an attempt to persuade" as the critical attribute of an argumentative essay, the student gives the answer "describes," you might respond, "The author certainly needs to describe his/her point of view and the evidence to support it in an argumentative essay. All of that is for a certain purpose. Listen carefully so you'll know that purpose." Then move on to a different student and come back either publicly or privately to the first student for repetition of the correct answer. "Because this is so important, we're going to go over it again."

At times, a student may give a completely irrelevant response either because (s)he is lost or because (s)he wants to "shake up" the class. If you believe the error is sincere and you can't think of any way to dignify it, you might say, "I'm not quite sure what you are thinking. Let's go on and see if it clears up for you." If you think the response is simply a bid for attention, it is best to ignore it and proceed to another student so you don't give the "clown" the attention desired.

You will note that in this chapter, we taught ways of productively correcting errors in their simplest forms. Then we introduced more complex forms and gave examples. Finally, we introduced the infrequent exception of its being occasionally correct to say, "No, you are wrong."

At first, using these techniques to deal with incorrect responses may seem cumbersome. "Who has time for all that?" you may ask. You will be surprised how automatic your enabling responses become as you practice using them with incorrect answers. There may be times when you tell a student, unequivocally, that (s)he is wrong. Most students, however, will participate more enthusiastically and will venture more responses in your class if they know that not only will you maintain their dignity but in doing so, but you'll also help them learn more and remember it longer—a major dividend from your skill in correcting incorrect answers.

# XIV  USING TIME TO ACHIEVE MORE LEARNING

Guide for Group Discussion or Individual Study

| | |
|---|---|
| **Objectives:** | *Participants will:*<br>a. State two ways to use time which otherwise could be wasted.<br>b. Design strategies which employ these techniques for future classes. |
| **Anticipatory Set:** | Identify times in your classes when time is wasted on matters that do not produce learning. |
| **Input & Modeling:** | Read the chapter and/or view the videotape, "Using Time To Achieve More Learning." |
| **Checking for Understanding & Guided Practice:** | a. Identify two ways to increase learning by using class time which otherwise would be wasted.<br>b. Apply these techniques to problems identified on your original list.<br>c. Generate examples of the use of these principles for your subsequent classes. |
| **Independent Practice:** | Try these techniques in subsequent classes to determine which are most effective. |

# USING TIME TO ACHIEVE MORE LEARNING

Time is the coin of teaching. That's what teachers have to spend to "buy" learning. We can invest time wisely in activities that result in students' learning, or we can fritter time away on inconsequential matters or in *waiting*.

When students are waiting (waiting for the class to convene, waiting for materials to be passed, waiting while roll is called, waiting for a turn), little learning is taking place. Sometimes waiting is inevitable, but lack of learning while waiting is not.

There are two ways you can change waiting time into learning time.

## I  Sponge activities

Sponge activities are learning activities that "sop up" precious time that otherwise would be lost. Sponge activities give students practice in reviewing or applying past learnings while they're waiting for students to arrive, while materials are being passed or collected, while roll is being taken, or during any other "administrivial" matters.

Sponge activities have two characteristics:

1. They are activities that accommodate late arrivals or early departures. A late arriving student must be able to "catch on" to what is going on as (s)he enters the room. Also, when you do not dismiss the whole class as a group, but "spin" them off to eliminate a traffic jam in getting materials, forming groups or dismissal, the sponge activity must not penalize the early departures.

2. Sponge activities review, giving practice or application of something already known. They do not introduce concepts or material new to the students.

Examples:

A. While waiting for all members of class to arrive, give an oral direction or one written on the chalkboard such as:

"Be ready to state three of the important differences we discussed yesterday between the continental shelf and the deep water of the ocean."

"Let's practice using the correct verb form in these sentences."

"See if you recall the authors of these lines."

"Give some synonyms for _____."

"Jot down a three sentence summary of yesterday's discussion."

"Solve this equation."

Verbal or written responses (which the teacher can walk around the room to examine) give an immediate diagnosis of what is understood and remembered and what needs to be retaught (with no papers to correct). Also, sponge activities give students needed practice in recalling and/or applying previous learning.

B. While taking roll or passing out papers and materials, ask a question of the group. Give them some time to think about the answer while you are checking a few names on the roll or giving back a few papers. Then call on a student you believe will answer correctly. This gives everyone the right answer with which to check his/her own response, and corrections can be made without public disclosure of error. If appropriate, ask the student who answered, or another student, to supply the reason for the validity of the answer. All during this time, you can be taking care of administrative tasks. Asking additional questions, giving thinking time and then calling on students for answers can give you whatever time is necessary for your teaching chores. Meanwhile, students are engaged in thinking and learning.

C. When dismissing students to gather materials or leave class, you frequently have a traffic jam. It is logistically and psychologically more sound to "spin off" a few at a time.

"While table one gets their materials, let's review the essential steps in the experiment."

"Explain your plan to your neighbor, and he or she will excuse you to gather your materials."

"Be ready to tell me the introductory sentence for your essay when I give you your paper."

"Signal me when you have decided on the three colors (events, characters, problem resolution, etc.) you will use, and I'll excuse you."

Use of inevitable waiting time for learning is limited only by your knowledge of what your class needs to practice or extend and by your own creativity. It is amazing how much students' learning and remembering can be increased through the use of sponge activities.

## II  Directing Questions to the Group

A second use of time which yields rich learning returns is the technique of addressing a question to the entire group so each student feels responsible for formulating an answer. This is in contrast to naming a student and then asking a question which frequently results in only the designated student thinking while the rest leave their minds in "idle" because the "pigeon has been picked for this one and it's not my responsibility." Consequently, it is an effective utilization of time to direct your question to the entire group for whom that question is appropriate.

Example:

"Be ready to tell me the four properties of _____. If you can think of only one, hold up one finger; indicate two by two fingers, etc." This questioning technique gives the teacher diagnostic information of "who knows how much."

Frequently, a teacher can have every student answer every question. Example:

"Read the first statement. Decide whether it is true or false. When I say, 'show me', make a plus or a minus with your fingers." or "Read the first question to yourself. Decide whether option 1, 2, 3 or 4 is the best answer and be ready to state why. When I say, 'show me', hold up that number of fingers."

Such questioning techniques not only stimulate each student to answer every question, but give the teacher essential diagnostic information of who knows what, whether the majority is certain or uncertain, and whether material is understood or needs to be retaught.

Obviously, the most important way to reap learning dividends from time expended is by excellence in teaching. If, in addition, you use techniques (sponge activities, beaming questions to the group rather than an individual, every student's signaling the answer) which glean learning from time which otherwise would be wasted, you will encourage students' maximum involvement and accomplishment in learning.

Use your own creativity to custom tailor these two techniques to your content, thereby increasing learning time in your own classroom.

# XV  TEACHING SO STUDENTS REMEMBER

Guide for Group Discussion or Individual Learning

**Objectives:**

*Participants will:*
a. Recall four factors which affect students' remembering what they have learned.
b. Generate examples of use of each factor in subsequent classes.
c. Practice incorporation of principles of retention in future plans for teaching.

**Anticipatory Set:**

List some techniques you use to help students remember what they have learned in your class.

**Input & Modeling:**

Read the chapter and/or view the videotape, "Teaching So Students Remember."

**Checking for Understanding & Guided Practice:**

a. List the four factors which promote retention, and examine your original list for examples of each.
b. Generate examples for any factor you omitted in your original list.
c. Develop examples of specific ways you can incorporate these four principles in subsequent classes.

**Independent Practice:**

Incorporate principles of retention in future classes. Determine which are most effective. Describe to your students what you are doing and encourage them to use these same techniques in their independent study.

# TEACHING SO STUDENTS REMEMBER

All of us have suffered the fallout of forgetting something we wanted to remember. We've also listened with dismay as our students assured us, "We've never had that!" when we distinctly remember teaching it.

Many factors which are beyond our control affect students' memory, and no one can guarantee remembering. There are, however, five factors we can incorporate in our teaching which substantially increase the probability that students will remember what they have learned in our classes.

You will recognize many of these factors from having read other chapters in this book. Excellence in instruction not only increases motivation to learn, but it increases the speed of learning and the probability of retention. Consequently, you'll find this chapter will be a useful review of many of the techniques you've already learned and, as a result, your memory of those techniques should increase.

## I Meaning

One of the most important factors which influences remembering either academic content, skills, or processes is the degree of meaning that particular learning had for the student. Chapter 8, "Making Material Meaningful," stressed the importance of using experiences from students' lives to illustrate the concept or generalization being taught. If we taught well in that chapter and our examples were meaningful, you will remember that meaning is not inherent in material but in the relationship of that material to students' own knowledge and past experience. When material is meaningful, it not only is learned more rapidly but it is remembered longer.

Examples:

"Suppose you rode your surfboard 200 ft."
    (for a Hawaiian student)
"Suppose you skied 200 ft. down a slope."
    (for a Colorado student)
"Suppose you planted 200 ft. of corn."
    (for an Iowa student)
"Suppose the gridiron was shortened to 200 ft."
    (for a football player)

The effective teacher takes the essence of what is being taught and translates it into students' knowledge and past experience. Not only does that make material more meaningful, but the example provides a reference point which will help the student recall the material when it is needed.

Examples:

"Suppose you wrote an argumentative essay to persuade me not to give a final exam. Let's look at the elements you would need to include," enables students to reach into their memory banks at a future time for the reference point of, "Oh yes, those were the elements that we included in our argument against the teacher giving a final," when they are trying to remember the elements of an effective argumentative essay.

"*Longitude* has the word *long* in it, with the 'l' pointing up and the 'g' pointing down, so you can remember it goes from top to bottom, from the 'top' of the world, the North Pole, to the 'bottom' of the world, the South Pole," gives the student the reference point of *long* is from top to bottom = *longitude*."

"You can remember that *dessert* is spelled with two s's because if you eat too much dessert, you'll get bigger around your middle. *Dessert* has more s's in its middle," brings something students already know to the current learning and gives them a reference point when they have to spell *dessert* or *desert*."

In each of these examples, something the student already knows or has experienced is brought forward by the teacher and connected to the new learning to be acquired. Old learning transfers from the past to the present and assists not only the speed of acquisition but the appropriate transfer of that new learning into a future situation when it is needed. You'll learn more about how to accomplish this transfer to future learning in the chapter on "Teaching for Transfer."

## II Feeling Tone

A second factor that promotes retention is feeling tone. You remember those things with which pleasant and unpleasant feelings are associated. When feelings are neutral, "it doesn't make any difference," it frequently doesn't make any difference if you remember it; so you don't. That material is forgotten.

We hope *you* remember, from the chapter on "Motivating Students to Learn," that pleasant feeling tones increase the learning effort that students put forth. Pleasant feeling tones also increase the probability that what was learned will be remembered. That is why we should try to make our classes pleasant, interesting, and our students successful.

Sometimes, we may want to interrupt pleasant feelings in order to raise students' level of concern about the importance of learning and remembering certain material which they will need in the future.

Consequently, we may introduce slightly unpleasant feeling tones. An excellent example of the function of unpleasant feeling tones in retention is the *wise* (not sadistic) use of tests.

Tests frequently are accompanied by the unpleasant feelings of accountability and evaluation. Consequently, tests can be an important aid to retention, particularly if 1) they're given frequently (so no one test is a life or death matter) and 2) students get immediate knowledge of results so they know if their answers are correct or incorrect and why. Effort to recall material is one of the best ways to practice that material. As a result, tests contribute a great deal to retention because they cause students to exert maximum effort to recall. Many short quizzes, only occasionally collected by the teacher, give a great deal of highly motivated practice and let students know what they have achieved and what they need to study.

Should the consequences of a test be so anxiety evoking that the student must use excessive energy to deal with the anxiety, there is little energy left for remembering. Those excessive feelings of concern may result in a test-phobic student who knows the material but can't remember it. Sometimes, to protect themselves, students need to deny the importance of the test and put forth no effort whatsoever in order to dilute unpleasant feelings until they become neutral. Neutral feeling tones may relieve tension, but they do nothing for retention. If "it doesn't matter," it usually won't be remembered.

Consequently, for maximum retention, students need to associate material and processes with pleasant feelings. Unpleasant feelings also are powerful, but they can have dangerous side effects. Neutral feeling tones are of no aid to retention.

### III Degree of original learning

A third factor that increases the probability of retention is students' achieving a high degree of original learning. We've all had the experience of meeting people and two minutes later, when we need to introduce them, find we've forgotten their names because we didn't learn them well in the first place.

Our teaching responsibility is to make sure that we provide students with the opportunity to achieve a high enough degree of learning so material will not easily be forgotten. (Not all students may avail themselves of that opportunity, but if we don't provide it, the fault is ours.) In Chapter 9, "Checking for Understanding," we suggest ways to insure a firm foundation so learning is secure and not easily forgotten. (Every chapter in this book will help you teach in a way that contributes to that foundation of learning.)

A caution to be sounded is "Don't just cover material." If you do, use a shovel, cover it with dirt, and lay it to rest, for that material will be dead as far as memory is concerned. If you don't have time to teach everything well, teach the most important concepts or processes to a high degree of learning. If you feel you must, assign the rest of the material to your students for independent learning (homework) so that what may not be learned well is least important.

## IV Schedule of Practice

Because students have learned something today is no guarantee they will remember it next week unless we incorporate in our instructional plan the power of a deliberate "schedule of practice" to achieve retention. From Chapter 10, "Designing Effective Practice," we hope *you* remember that massing practice, many short, intense practice periods close together, makes for fast learning and a high degree of original learning. However, even though something may be well learned, if it is not used it can be forgotten. Consequently, once something has been learned, we need to increase the probability of its retention by changing the practice schedule from "massed" to "distributed" practice. Distributed practice means that material is periodically reviewed but with longer and longer time intervals between reviews. Distributed practice makes for very durable learning that is "forgetting resistant."

We frequently assume that our students are conscientious and will distribute their own practice by doing homework, rereading and/or reviewing. If we explain to them why this is necessary for their remembering what they have learned, and we also occasionally *model the value of distributed practice* by reviewing material in class, students' asumption of responsibility for their own distributed practice will more predictably occur.

Use "odds and ends" of time in your class to review previous learning. For example, while your class is assembling, or preparing to leave, when you're passing back or collecting papers, or when you have unavoidable delays (the projector bulb has burned out or you're waiting for a speaker, for a film, bell, students, books, tests, etc.); practice something that needs periodic review. Chapter 14, "Using Time to Achieve More Learning," suggests several ways to use those tag ends of time for distributed practice. By doing so, you will make a major contribution to your students' remembering.

In this chapter, you have read about four factors you can use to increase students' retention of what they have learned: 1) meaning, 2) feeling tone, 3) degree of original learning, and 4) practice schedule. These factors are not discrete; they interact. We separate them only to bring each to your attention. By deliberately incorporating each factor in your teaching, you can contribute immeasurably to your students' successful remembering what they have learned.

## V Transfer

The last factor that can promote or interfere with retention is the phenomenon of *transfer of learning*. Past learning can transfer to the present and block retrieval of something you wish to remember. (You keep recalling your friend's maiden name when you want to remember her married name.) Past learning also can transfer to the present and not only facilitate present learning but can be the springboard for all future problem solving, decision making, and creativity.

*Transfer* is so important that our next chapter will focus on the ways you can encourage transfer. Also, by deliberately utilizing teaching principles that promote transfer, you will be able to take what you have learned in this book and from the *Mastery Teaching Videotapes* and transfer that learning to your increasingly effective future teaching.

# XVI  TEACHING FOR TRANSFER

## Guide for Group Discussion or Individual Study

**Objectives:**
*Participants will:*
a. Identify four factors that promote transfer.
b. Generate examples using those factors in their own content area.
c. Plan for future class sessions which incorporate the propulsion of transfer theory.

**Anticipatory Set:**
What factors in teaching promote transfer of learning to new situations?

**Input & Modeling:**
Read the chapter and/or view the videotape, "Teaching for Transfer."

**Checking for Understanding & Guided Practice:**
a. Identify four factors that promote transfer.
b. Recall examples of errors that are the result of students' perceiving things as similar and develop discriminators that emphasize differences.
c. Generate examples which emphasize similarity of students' previous knowledge to new learnings in subsequent classes.
d. Identify associations students bring to your content area. Develop ways of changing nonproductive associations and strengthening productive ones.
e. Develop indices of adequate degrees of original learning and determine how you will secure evidence that your students have achieved to that level.
f. Identify critical attributes of subsequent instructional content and determine how your students will identify and learn those attributes.

**Independent Practice:**
Try these ideas in subsequent classes and identify those ideas which are most productive. Remember, an excellent idea or technique often needs modification and polishing before it becomes an element of artistic teaching.

# TEACHING FOR TRANSFER

Transfer is one of the most powerful principles of learning. Transfer is the process of past learning influencing the acquisition of new learning. Transfer is the basis of all creativity, problem solving, and the making of satisfying decisions. In addition to these important functions, transfer can dramatically shorten or lengthen the time it takes to acquire new learning.

Transfer is a more reliable predictor of speed of new learning than is I.Q. As an example, one student spends most of his time reading *Road and Track* with his head under the hood of the car, tearing down the engine. A second student with the same I.Q. spends most of his time reading Shakespeare. Which student will more rapidly learn the carburetion system of a new automobile? It's obvious, isn't it? Suppose the first student had the lower I.Q.. Would you change your opinion? Of course not. It's also obvious that the second student would more rapidly learn the meaning of English words of the 16th century, not because he is brighter but because he already has a lot of previous learning that can transfer into the new learning task.

In a similar way, Edison, Michaelangelo, and the astronauts had acquired a great deal of knowledge and skill to transfer into their performance. Certainly, ability played a role in their success but other humans of equal ability could not have achieved in the same way unless they also had the prerequisite learning necessary for the transfer that made achievement possible. This process of old learning accelerating the acquisition of new learning is called *positive transfer.*

Transfer of old learnings is not always positive. Old learnings can interferer with the acquisition of new learning and result in confusion or errors. When old learning interferes with new learning, it is called *negative transfer.* As an example, once you have learned to pronounce the English word *robe,* it is more difficult to pronounce that word correctly when you see it written in the French sentence "C'est une robe." Because students learn an apostrophe can indicate possession, that knowledge may transfer negatively and result in their writing, "It's leg was broken." If previous teachers have required students to memorize and regurgitate material, we find it more difficult to encourage students to do their own thinking rather than to parrot what the teacher or the book said.

To utilize the learning propulsion from positive transfer and minimize the interference of negative transfer, it is important we identify the factors that stimulate transfer and, in our teaching, deliberately incorporate those which will facilitate student learning and performance and eliminate or minimize those factors that could cause interference.

Diagrammatically expressed, we can affect only the present, but in that present we can "hook" into past learning experiences and pull that learning forward to facilitate present learning. We "cut it off" to prevent the interference of negative transfer. We teach to increase the positive transfer of present learning to future situations where it is appropriate and minimize negative transfer to a future situation where that learning would be inappropriate.

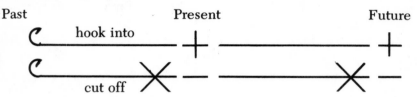

Four factors in a learning situation can promote transfer. No one is most important, and often they operate in concert. By becoming aware of each of them, we can enhance positive transfer and minimize negative transfer as we teach.

## I Similarity

Whenever two learnings have an element or elements that appear to the learner as similar, it is more probable that one learning will transfer into the other. The similarity may be perceived, 1) in the environment, 2) in the way the learner feels or thinks, or 3) in the mode of attack or learning methodology being employed. As an obvious example of similarity of environment, when a student learns to use the library to locate material for an English class, those skills transfer into the new task of locating material for a science class. Even though the content is different, the perception of the library as a source of information and the mode of attack are the same.

Perceptions of similarity can also lead to negative transfer. Twins are perceived as similar so one is called by the other's name. Students confuse *mitosis* and *miosis*, *latitude* and *longitude* because of similarity.

Ways of feeling or thinking transfer. Notice the feelings you transfer from your past to the present when you read these chapters. Some of you are transferring feelings of "I always wanted to know more about how to teach effectively." Others are transferring (with a groan) feelings of "Something else I have to learn," or "Who doesn't know that?" Some of you are transferring your typical style of thinking analytically. Others are transferring their more holistic style and are concerned that analytic thinking may destroy creativity.

An English professor and a statistician would transfer different ways of thinking to their reading of a research article in a professional journal. The statistician would be looking at the validity with which results had been interpreted and could be substantiated. The English professor would be thinking about organization, clarity of presentation, and word usage.

Students transfer previous ways of thinking into their present classes. When a course requires a very different way of thinking, changing from analytic to holistic, from concrete to abstract, from one right answer to many different answers, from one way of organizing language to a new way, negative transfer can result from the similarity of "taking a course," "writing papers," "sitting in the classrooms," "getting grades." The old mode of thinking or feeling transfers into and interferes with new performance expectations.

On the other hand, once a student learns how to think analytically, that skill does not have to be relearned for the next class that requires it. Once a student has learned to deal productively with abstractions, that thinking skill can be transferred to new situations which are perceived as similar.

Sometimes the similarity of the past learning to the present is in the mode of attack. "Can you remember?" elicits the behavior of reaching into a "memory bank," a strategy different from the response to "Can you figure out?" or "Could you possibly imagine?"

Because similarity promotes transfer, we need to emphasize that similarity when the transfer will be positive. "The French word for red is *rouge* which is the *same* word we use for the red color women put on their cheeks and lips." "This problem is similar to the one you handled so effectively last week," encourages a perplexed student to transfer successful problem solving skills.

If the similarity will promote negative transfer we keep the two learnings separate. Don't teach *latitude* and *longitude* on the same day. When two learnings become confused, we emphasize the difference. "Unlike English, the modifier comes *after* the noun in French. We say 'red hat': Unlike us, they say 'chapeau rouge.'"

There is no way that this short chapter can explore all the possibilities for eliciting positive transfer and minimizing negative transfer as a result of similarity of two learnings. We hope that your reading will generate enough interest so that looking for similarities will transfer into continuing investigation of their potential in teaching effectiveness.

## II Association

Whenever two events, feelings or actions occur together in time, they can become associated, "bonded" or welded together, so the presence of one elicits the recall of the other. "Romeo" elicits "Juliet." "Statistics" usually elicit the feeling "never again." "Pavlov" elicits "conditioning." Even though there is no similarity between the two items, they have occurred together so they become associated.

This bonding is especially powerful for feelings that have become associated with concepts or environments. Look at the feelings you have bonded to the concepts of "communism," "motherhood," "slums," "science," "poetry", "final exams." Because of the transfer power of such association, we want to bond our content and classroom experiences with students' feelings of interest, competence, and successful achievement so meeting that content in the future will elicit feelings of, "I am competent in that area and I really enjoy it." This book and series of videotapes were produced to facilitate the bonding of your efforts to become increasingly effective with the satisfaction derived from your students' accelerating achievement.

Simulation is one way of increasing students' perception of similarity and bonding appropriate actions to significant cues in the environment. Fire drills utilize the similarity of an auditory signal, regardless of the difference of other factors in the environment, and bond that signal to the response of an orderly evacuation. Simulation at the NASA Space Center transferred to the completely new experience of a near perfect moon landing. As we anticipate skills and information needed by our students in future situations, simulations of those situations (interviews, experiments, examinations, problem situations) will increase the probability that what we are teaching will transfer appropriately into the future.

We also need to use examples from the students' own experiences, emphasizing the similarity of what they already know, understand, and have experienced so it will transfer approximately to new learning. For example if we're teaching base six in math (heaven knows why), we can hook into students' knowledge of soft drinks and use as example single cans, six packs, and a carton of six six packs. The selection of the examples we use is such a powerful propellent to learning that the chapter, "Making Material Meaningful," has been devoted to that important element of effective teaching.

### III Degree of original learning

Whatever is well learned will transfer more appropriately into the future than will poorly or insufficiently learned skills or material. Clearly, a student who barely understands the scientific process is not going to do acceptable research. The student who has just begun to work with clay will not produce a masterpiece. The student who is a beginner in basketball will not score the most points. These students have not acquired a high enough degree of learning to transfer their skills dependably and predictably into future successful performances.

If something is worth teaching, it is worth teaching well. While achieving an adequate degree of learning is a responsibility of the learner, contributing to that adequacy is also a primary responsibility of the instructor. It is to help you fulfill that responsibility that this book and series of videotapes were produced.

Transfer is not always within our control. But with careful planning plus scientific and artistic instruction, we can identify similarities when they will contribute to positive transfer and emphasize differences when we do not wish that transfer to occur. Effective and artistic teaching also will increase the probability that your students' interest and success will become associated with your subject field, and a higher degree of learning will be achieved. Still, there are factors beyond our control that also can influence the perception of similarity, association, and degree of learning. A student may perceive some element of our class as similar to something that caused him difficulty in the past. Also absence, lack of effort, or aptitude can result in an inadequate degree of learning.

There is a fourth factor that promotes positive transfer which can be completely within our control. That factor is identification of the critical attribute that makes something what is and thereby more nearly guarantees appropriate transfer of current learning into future situations where that learning can appropriately be applied.

### IV Critical attributes

Critical attributes are those attributes which differentiate one thing from another. A critical attribute of a mammal is that it has mammary glands. There are other attributes possessed by mammals such as being warm blooded and having an internal skeleton, but those attributes do not distinguish mammals from birds or reptiles. A critical attribute of a topic sentence is that it presents the generalization which all the other sentences support or develop. It has other essential elements, such as a subject and a predicate, but those do not distinguish it from other sentences.

The power of a critical attribute is that, once identified, it can be applied to any new situation to confirm or deny the applicability of previous knowledge to that new, never before encountered situation. This application is the launching pad for problem solving, decision making and creativity.

While we may encourage students to discover critical attributes, most of the time we should plan to teach those attributes and let students' discovery be the identification of those attributes in new situations. To teach a critical attribute we need to:

1. *Identify the attribute which makes something what it is—not always an easy or, in some cases, even a possible task.*

   For example, what attribute(s) differentiates an explorer from a conqueror, a pioneer, a trespasser or from a nosy person? Common attributes could be curiosity, initiative, courage, fortitude, perseverance, but the critical attributes are, 1) penetration of an area unknown to the explorer, 2) by actions condoned by the explorer's society, 3) for the primary purpose of securing information. These three critical attributes eliminate conquerors (primary purpose is conquest), people who are lost (primary purpose is to get back home), trespassers, and nosy persons (not condoned by their society).

2. *Cite simple and obvious examples.*

   Examples should be carefully selected in advance by the teacher. *Don't ask students for examples when you introduce a critical attribute.* Students have an absolute gift for volunteering murky or confusing examples or those which present an exception to the rule.

   "Columbus was an explorer because he was seeking information as to whether a vessel could arrive in the east by sailing west, a voyage his society sanctioned."

   "Napoleon was not an explorer because even though he went into lands new to him, his primary purpose was conquest, not information."

3. *Cite more complex examples.*

   "The U.S. astronauts were funded by their country to explore the surface of the moon, record data, and bring back specimens for scientific investigation; but their voyage also fulfilled the purpose of demonstrating the scientific supremacy of the United States."

   Only after students can apply the critical attribute to discriminate between simple and then more complex exemplars and nonexemplars, should they be encouraged to generate their own examples.

4. *Students generate examples.*

At this point, students should be ready to transfer their knowledge into the generation of examples which do and do not satisfy the criteria set by the critical attribute(s). This process should increase the probability that in the future they will be able to transfer the discriminator, skill, concept, or generalization approximately to new learning, problem solving, decision making or creative endeavor.

5. *Teach the limits of the critical attribute.*

Aggravating exceptions to rules, generalizations, categories and critical attributes seem to emerge just when we think we "truly understand." It seems that the critical attribute of "truly understanding" is the recognition that there is always more to know. While it is appropriate to state at the beginning "there are exceptions," those exceptions should not be introduced until a basic understanding is acquired and can be applied appropriately to new situations. Teaching a rule and its exceptions at the same time results in confusion and an inadequate degree of original learning and therefore faulty transfer of that learning to future situations.

Teaching for transfer is the hallmark of effectiveness and artistry in our profession. If, after reading this chapter and viewing the videotape, you feel you need to learn a great deal more about transfer, congratulate yourself on your professional sensitivity. Transfer is a very complex concept and one on which the most sophisticated teachers are expending a great deal of time and thought.

If you plan your instruction to emphasize similarities that encourage positive transfer, associate students' successful achievement with your content area, use this book and the *Mastery Learning Videotapes* to increase your teaching effectiveness so students achieve a high degree of original learning and you identify the critical attributes of the skills, concepts, and generalizations that you teach so your students can successfully transfer their knowledge to new situations, we will have achieved transfer of the basic concepts of *Mastery Teaching* to your increasingly excellent professional performance.